MY LOVE AFFAIR WITH BARACK OBAMA

some occasional writings

by Peter Breschard

also by Peter Breschard

CIRCUS RIDER
IN THE WIND
IMELDA AND FRIENDS
DEAD LEPERS

GALLDUBH PRESS
4584 SENECA DRIVE
OKEMOS, MI 48864
Galldubh@aol.com
www.CircusRider.org

WHO BENEFITS MOST FROM CORPORATE PERSONHOOD?

Now that Senator Bernie Sanders has collected over 109,000 electronic signatures in support of the Saving American Democracy Amendment, which would help restore the definition of citizens as being human beings, you might ask yourself why you haven't heard about Sanders' amendment in any newspaper or newsgroup, or on the radio, or on national television.

With all the brouhaha over five Supreme Court justices deciding that corporations, a legal concept, deserve the rights and privileges of an American citizen; one of the interesting aspects of this product of deranged minds remains; who profits from such an Escher-like contortion of freedom of speech?

Let's face it, corporations are incapable of thought, and the Four Supremes Plus One seems to have as much interest in the rights of American citizens as you would find in an early prototype of Babbage's Analytical Engine.

You might think corporations have been given this pseudo-citizenship in order for them to control the United States government. Think again. For the most part corporations aren't designed to plan that far in advance. Corporations are intrinsically conservative, not radical. Virtually any change costs businesses money, so it's in their DNA to be change adverse. So why the drive for corporate personhood?

Ever wonder who sets the conversation for the American dinner table? (If that still exists.) Since you're reading this, you probably read various news sources in print and on the web but you also listen to, or watch, the tubes and be they Fox cryptos or Rachel, Lawrence, or Ed, the political conversation is pretty much dictated by these professional pundits and their questionable news sources.

How do these scribbling, talking heads earn their money? Why do all of them consider news to be how many times Newt Gingrich farts in the face of Mitt Romney? Why distract the informed citizen with daily insignificant political nonsense when something as essential to the American way of life as Bernie Sanders' Saving American Democracy Amendment receives almost no coverage at all?

Getting back to the earlier question, the organizations that directly profit the most from corporate personhood are the for-profit media networks. What has been created is a constant election cycle which demands constant partisan advertisements.

Any good ad salesman has a general idea of their client's advertising budget. What happened with the Four Supremes Plus One decisions that speech=cash and corporations=people, was that the political advertising budgets for corporations were transfigured from Pound Puppies to Wicked Wild Wolves. Media corporations realized that corporate personhood meant corporations were now free to purchase infinite hours of pro-corporate advertisements.

Do you think that the media outlets want to cut their own throats? Do you think that Rachel's, and Ed's, and Bill's producers aren't informed by their superiors that covering Bernie Sanders' Saving American Democracy Amendment is actually cutting their own throats?

Remember as you consider whatever distraction MSNBC, CNN, the New York Times, Fox, ABC, NBC, etc., presents you for the day, that all these outlets live on advertising revenue and Bernie Sanders' Saving American Democracy Amendment would slay their golden egg laying geese.

SUNDAY, DECEMBER 11, 2011

PETER BRESCHARD

ARE YOU A CRIMINAL OR A VICTIM?

There's a bit of a thief in all of us. Human beings are capable of attempting whatever deed any other human being has attempted, and can conceive of unspeakable actions without ever carrying a single one of them out.

Right now, the vast majority of people in the United States are engaged, to one degree or another, in a criminal enterprise. During Prohibition the vast majority of citizens were involved in a criminal enterprise as well. From homicidal gang lord to neighborhood bartender, when booze was illegal all those in the liquor business were involved in the same criminal enterprise. What mattered was what degree of culpability was involved. A bellboy who dropped a bottle off at your hotel room was not as culpable as an investment banker financing boatloads of booze coming across the border.

Profiting by withholding medical care from human beings in need is a criminal act. Denial of basic human rights for profit has a long and despicable history in the United States. Denial for profit of one human right, liberty, was known as slavery. Denial of medical care for profit is known as America's current health insurance system.

Who are the victims and who are the criminals?

When a citizen takes twenty percent of their monthly disposable income and signs it over to a for-profit insurance company in order to protect their physical, mental, and fiscal well being; is that person a criminal or a victim?

When a citizen receives one hundred percent of their monthly income by investing in a company which earns a majority of its profits by withholding medical assistance to those unable to meet their price; is that person a criminal or a victim?

These are two minor examples of participants in the same criminal enterprise. Both engage in monetary transactions with organizations involved in the withholding of medical care. But one of them is a victim in that a virtual gun is being held to their head. Your money or your health, mind, and/or property. In the current situation, not buying into the criminal healthcare network puts individual citizens in great jeopardy of not receiving adequate medical attention and treatment when necessary and of losing all of one's property if not sufficiently covered.

An individual forced to pay into a criminal enterprise is a victim.

There are also those citizens who are the equivalent of slave traders. These people are involved with the for-profit healthcare system for the purpose of extracting wealth from the withholding from their fellow citizens of a basic human right. Within the USA these people act as simple extortionists whose motto might as well be, "Your money or your health."

An individual who intentionally inflicts harm on a fellow citizen, and who profits financially by doing so, is a criminal.

Most American citizens fall somewhere between these two extremes within the criminal enterprise which is healthcare in the United States. A part-time medical secretary at a community hospital is certainly less culpable than an investor in a medical office which specializes in Medicare fraud. But just by dealing with the present system, we all have blood on our hands to a greater or lesser degree.

And this is what the real criminals want you to feel. They want you to think that if you're in for a penny you're in for a pound. That we are all criminals like them.

Rubbish.

If all you do is try and survive and you feel the necessity of purchasing a policy from a for-profit medical insurance company, you aren't a criminal, you are a victim of the criminal enterprise.

If all you do is invest your money in companies who profit from withholding medical treatment from those in need, you aren't a victim, you are a criminal and a willing participant in a criminal enterprise.

There is a continuum here which stretches from victim to criminal predator.

Most are victims.

Many are criminals.

THURSDAY, DECEMBER 1, 2011

OCCUPY WHERE THE
MONEY IS

George went down to the local Occupation camp the other day. You have to understand, George doesn't live in a big city. George lives in what people in big cities hardly would consider a city at all. But his hometown is a state capital and as such has an Occupation going on.

Now George's mayor pulled a smart move when the Occupation first began. George's mayor welcomed the Occupation with open arms and even provided park space where they could camp and not be hassled by the local gendarmes. George's mayor said he agreed with the objectives of the Occupation movement and all seemed to be well with the world.

Well, it turns out the park where the Occupation planted its stakes is almost too nice. Everybody put up their tents and marched around for a couple of weeks and now the Occupation in George's city is where it is.

The Occupation in George's city is pretty much out of sight and out of mind. By parking the Occupation camp where he parked the Occupation camp, George's mayor guaranteed that most of the people in his city wouldn't be subjected to any aggravation by the Occupation. The folks who now live in the Occupation camp, among a whole bunch of empty tents, are trying to maintain while not being a nuisance to the citizens of George's city.

Location. Location. Location.

Would Occupy Wall Street have worked as well as it has if it had been Occupy Staten Island? For those of you not familiar with the geography of New York City, Wall Street is the heart of the financial world and Staten Island has been referred to by many as a sleepy suburb. Now they're both New York City but if Occupation Wall Street had been Occupation Staten Island, you wouldn't be reading this and this wouldn't have been written.

The Occupation in George's city is now located in what could best be called a sleepy suburb. Out of sight, out of mind.

George's city used to be a manufacturing city. That was where the money was. But that work is mostly gone now. Now George's city is has two large employers. The State and a State University. Now the State capital, close to where George's Occupation camp now is, employs a lot of people making good but not Wall Street money. Strangely enough, the State University employs a number of people making Wall Street numbers of over half a million dollars a year. (Which is odd because they all sort of work for the governor of the State who is paid a whole lot less than that.)

Plus there are all the students who might join the Occupation if the Occupation weren't in the middle of what might as well be a sleepy suburb.

George is going to mention that his local Occupation should stop occupying the sleepy suburb and start occupying the State University because George thinks that's where they should have been to start.

Occupy where the money is.

SATURDAY, NOVEMBER 19, 2011

BROOKS BROTHERS T-SHIRT

SPECIAL EVENT

Every thirteen years Brooks Brothers conducts a very special T-shirt event for our most favored clients. These high thread count wonders are woven from the begrimed souls of corporate CEOs, and other club members, who have gone on to the ultimate tax haven during the intervening years. The Brothers Brooks, serving their clientele from cradle to grave and possibly beyond, long ago purchased options on these doomed spirits during various business school mixers early on in these globe striding business tycoons' careers.

Luxurious to the touch yet wonderfully dependable in their strength and endurance, these solidly superior garments are the soul threads of corporate America. Woven with fibers softened by the tears and sorrows of billions of victims, these textile testaments to our globalized economy amass a residual strength through the echoes of market famines, oil wars, for-profit health care death machines, privatized torture, and the ever useful fear of homelessness.

Wrap yourself in the empty dreams of dead bottom line types, those who knew the market would correct for everything. Become enshrouded in the despair of new cadavers whose favorite line remains "the money is all green" even as they discover just how many rings of hell there actually are.

Brooks Brothers is proud to present these ultimate in prestige T-shirts for a limited time only.

****

"Keep your friends close, but your enemies closer."
- Michael Corleone

****

THURSDAY, OCTOBER 13, 2011

VOTE FOR OBAMA!

After he arrests Bush

Vote for Obama after he arrests Bush. Not before.

Not when he starts an investigation which will drag on until after the Presidential election and possibly disappear afterwards.

Vote for Obama when he stops ignoring and violating the law.

Vote for Obama when he jettisons the precedent he is currently setting of allowing those who authorized the torture of powerless prisoners to escape all legal consequences.

Vote for Obama when he follows the law of the United States of America and puts George W. Bush, self-confessed torturer, behind bars.

"Justice delayed is justice denied."

No matter what reason President Obama may have, he is currently in violation of the law by not prosecuting his predecessor.

The United Nations Convention Against Torture not only obliges its signatories to investigate and prosecute those who commit torture, it views those who are in power to prosecute and who do not do so as being as culpable as those they are protecting.

It is now too late in the game to vote for Obama if he only begins an investigation of those who disgraced the United States by ordering the torture of prisoners. In the last few days various voices have been praising President Obama for his progressive utterances. Many of those disappointed over the past few years by the Republican programs which President Obama has been pursuing, are once again hoping for hope. They assume President Obama has some credibility. After being fooled once, they are doubling down.

Guantanamo is still in operation.

Tens of thousands of troops are in Iraq.

No job program has been implemented.

Americans will soon be forced to purchase medical insurance from for-profit medical insurance companies where lives are viewed as debits or credits.

Self-confessed torturers are allowed to walk free.

If President Obama wishes to once again become a credible human being, there is one thing he can do.

Barack Obama must stop being a war criminal and arrest George W. Bush for crimes against humanity.

After President Obama arrests George W. Bush is when you should vote for Barack Obama for President.

Not before.

TUESDAY, SEPTEMBER 20, 2011

WHEN SHOULD PHIL RESIGN AS DOG CATCHER?

Don't the howls wake you up in the morning? I know they do me. And I'm pretty sure that those packs of rabid dogs growling and prowling around Phil's house probably wake him and his family up as well. Rabid dogs taking control of the streets means the problem has gotten out of hand.

Like I've said before, Phil is a swell guy and if I were in college I'm sure I'd really enjoy taking one of his classes on the history of Dog Catching but right now theory just isn't getting a whole bunch of jobs done.

I have a pretty good idea what you're going to say. The folks who are putting up a candidate to oppose Phil don't want whoever holds the position of Dog Catcher to do anything at all. They say that if it were up to them there wouldn't even be a Dog Catcher. If you don't vote for Phil you're just letting those who want rabid dogs to run totally free win. And nobody in their right minds wants that.

Phil, resign now and let us run somebody else.

Back when I was a teenager there was a big project I wanted to do. So, one morning I rolled up my sleeves and got to work. By the end of the afternoon, you could see I'd done a lot of work. There were parts and tools all over the place. But as I stood there looking out over a good day's work, I realized something. I realized I was way over my head and really had no idea what I was doing. It wasn't that the job was beyond my intellect. It simply was that I had no idea what I was doing. It went against my grain to realize that I should quit the job and let someone with more experience and talent take over, but that's what I did. One of the smartest moves I ever made in my life.

Some people can sing. Some can't. Some folks can play contract bridge or chess like wizards. Others have no interest or talent. Some folks can sail a boat. Others send themselves and their passengers on a one way tour of Davy Jones' Locker.

The famous Dutch Woman
La fameuse Hollandoise Danceuse de Corde

GK 4107

Phil, take a look around you. The dogs are running wild. You've spent all the money allotted to your department. You must know by now that you couldn't catch a dog if your life depended on it.

Phil, it's time for you to resign.

I know it's an ego thing on your part. You know you should be able to be a Dog Catcher and that people with a lot less mental capacity than you have managed to be reasonably good Dog Catchers.

That's life.

Phil, you really suck at the job. It's time for you to give it up.

This doesn't mean that we all don't like you. It's just that we really should find something else for you to do. Something a bit more suited to your talents.

Thank you.

WEDNESDAY, AUGUST 10, 2011

WHY PHIL SHOULDN'T BE ELECTED DOG CATCHER

Phil shouldn't be elected dog catcher.

Some folks should never get anywhere near a carburetor either. Or a fuel pump. Or a radiator. Or a transmission. You pick whatever part of an automobile you want and some folks shouldn't touch it with a ten-foot long socket wrench.

Now, let's get something straight right from the jump. Phil is one hell of a smart fellow. As far as brains packed into cubic centimeters, you're not going to find a brighter bulb if you searched all around for a month.

Phil knows his history. He knows philosophy. He's studied politics. He's even taught law. You're not going to fault the guy on the academic side, that's for sure.

And personable? You bet. He's got a smile and a set of teeth which could send the hearts of an entire convention of orthodontists all atwitter. Phil can make a whole room happy just by walking into it. There's probably not a digit big enough to describe the number of mothers who imagined Phil with their daughters.

Phil is an extremely intelligent, well studied, personable, charming guy.

Which might be part of the reason he shouldn't be elected dog catcher.

Just like people with absolutely no experience as mechanics shouldn't be paid to put a wrench to an engine, Phil really shouldn't be elected to the post of dog catcher.

Maybe it has something to do with getting your hands dirty. Phil just isn't the kind of guy to actually be able to do the job. Why? Good question. Have any of you ever seen Phil with a dog? He certainly has made a lot of speeches, but nobody has ever come forward and claimed that they've actually ever seen Phil within twenty feet of a dog. If you're going to be the dog catcher around here, you've really got to get a lot closer to the animals than Phil ever has been. You can't deliver a lot of feel good speeches and expect a pack of rabid dogs to lock themselves up in a cage without any human intervention.

You have to get your hands dirty. You've got to go running after the dogs and throw a net over them. You've got to bring those curs down. You've got to break into a sweat and face a pack of bared fangs that want to rip your throat apart. You have to get out of the office, lose your cool, and get down and dirty with a pack of wild dogs.

Phil, as we've all seen, is incapable of any of that.

Just like you wouldn't let any fool with no experience work on your car, you shouldn't elect Phil dog catcher.

Some folks say because he was elected dog catcher last election we should elect him this time around.

But the question remains, has anyone ever seen Phil anywhere near a dog?

Don't elect Phil again.

Are you better off with all those rabid dogs running around?

Don't elect Phil dog catcher again.

Thank you.

TUESDAY, AUGUST 2, 2011

MERE MINDLESSNESS

And so the blather which presents itself as statesmanship continues. The party of the extreme right dithers on about no government while the party of the less extreme right wing weeps about how it will have to take even more money from the poor and hand it over to their immensely wealthy donors.

If Obama or Boehner had a balanced budget and all the discretionary cash in the world, they wouldn't know what to do with it because neither of them have a brain in their heads when it comes to what this country should actually be doing. Both Obama and Boehner are obsessed about counting the pennies in this country's household change jar.

For months what has been dominating the media streams is the debt ceiling. The debt ceiling is a mundane piece of crap, as any twelve year-old lemonade stand owner can tell you. How did raising the debt ceiling, something so routine that it's been done over one hundred times before, become the latest performance piece for drama queens Obama and Boehner?

It plays like this. Boehner, as head of the opposition, has to choose a position opposite that of Obama yet still be within the Republican party play book. Problem: Obama has stolen all the moderate and conservative plays and is running them himself. Boehner is stuck with the extreme conservative play book because that's the only part of the Republican party Obama isn't already representing.

Which is pretty bad for Boehner but great for Obama since all Obama cares about is getting reelected anyway. And it's pretty damn horrible for the country when in the midst of a depression a Democratic president is cutting social programs. 10% unemployment and the Democrats are talking cuts. Remember, it was Obama who signed the extension of the Bush tax giveaways to the wealthiest Americans. Would we be in such dire straits if Obama hadn't signed that extension? And no more friggin whining! The Republicans made me do it! Pitiful. The President of the United States of America has the biggest Bully Pulpit in the world and all we hear from the current Chief Executive is why he can't do anything. Pitiful.

Right now the President should be promoting a two million person job bill and the Republicans should be whining how it should only be a one million person job bill.

Right now the President should be sending to congress an infrastructure bill to top all infrastructure bills and the Republicans should be whining how their districts aren't getting a big enough piece of the pie.

Right now the President should be prosecuting those who ordered the torture of prisoners in the name of the United States and the Republicans should be hiring lawyers and resigning.

Instead Obama and Boehner are playing footsies with each other and counting the future votes.

A pox on both of them.

SATURDAY, JULY 30, 2011

ERSATZ, OR NOT ERSATZ?

And now a brief pause.

Bin Laden is dead. No tears were shed. Moving on.

Days after the incumbent president officially announces his hat is now in the ring for reelection, the fugitive is found and killed.

Three wars.

There is time to look back and execute the terrorist but there is no time to look back and prosecute the self-confessed torturer and his cronies.

Mr. Obama is a consummate politician.

The unions no longer back this incumbent with the same mindless tenacity as they once did. Many unionists believe the Democratic Party is now run by what were once called moderate Republicans. They are surprised that the Democrats act as if they are controlled by the same pro-corporate interests as the Republicans. Others are not so surprised.

Out of the West arises a Mormon. Jon Meade Huntsman, Jr. is the scariest Republican to enter the national scene in a very long time. Aside from being a billionaire, extremely well respected in his own state, and a resume which is just this side of

tremendous, Mr. Huntsman is something President Obama has always wanted to be, a moderate Republican.

Will the nation back the ersatz moderate Republican, Obama, when a real moderate Republican is on the same ballot?

Will the nation seek to repeat a similar thrill to that of electing the first Irish-Kenyan American to the nation's highest office by electing the first Mormon?

The Republican Party has shown itself to be a mindless herd of rabid sheep when its right wing is allowed free reign. Mr. Obama knows this, which is why for his entire administration he has promoted moderate Republican policies. He has left the present Republicans with no breathing space. In order to mount an opposition, the Republicans have been driven to feed upon themselves as they maneuver to the extreme right. This is brilliant politics; but, as we all know by now, even moderate Republican policy is disasterous for the American people.

Enter Mr. Huntsman.

American voters will usually elect real Republicans when faced with the choice between a moderate Republican and a Democrat who is also brought to you by your local Chamber of Commerce. Obama is no Democrat. He is, however, the person who may be responsible for selling the largest number of private medical insurance policies ever. Not to mention shoveling a dollar or two into the rapacious paws of Wall Street.

Will America vote for the real Republican bastard, Huntsman; or will they stay with the ersatz Republican Obama? Time and a pile of more dead bodies will tell.

SUNDAY, MAY 22, 2011

OBAMA AS THE REINCARNATION OF BOB DOLE

Obama supporters are like prisoners who are proud of their large cell.

TUESDAY, APRIL 26, 2011

SELF-MADE NOBODIES

Self-made American billionaires.

You have to be kidding.

Self-made men, that's what America is all about.

Rubbish.

One person, raising themself up by their own bootstraps, and making a fortune single handedly. It's the American way.

You are kidding, aren't you?

Let's analyze the myth of self-made wealth in the United States.

Begin at the beginning.

Bill Gates, Warren Buffett, Oprah Winfrey, John D. Rockefeller, et al, what do they all have in common?

Aside from some spare simoleons, these allegedly self-made wunderkinds were all lottery winners. They were all lottery winners at birth. They were born in the United States of America whereas they could as easily have been born to Inuit families somewhere north of north. John D.'s fortune might have been severely handicapped if the closest oil he could have put his hands on were Canadian shale oil reserves. And that's just luck by geography.

Ever use a dollar bill?

Of course you have. So have Gates, Buffett, Winfrey, and Rockefeller.

Consider the dollar bill for a moment or so.

A promissary note backed by the full faith and credit of the United States government.

Dollar bills are contracts. Use these and we promise they'll be worth something. The U.S. government, Gates, Buffett, Winfrey, and Rockefeller were partners to the same contract whenever a dollar bill changed hands.

Every dollar bill in the bank is a contract with the American people. It's not individual's money. All a dollar bill is is a contract backed by the American people.

Self-made billionaires.

Sure, pal. And there's a bridge in Brooklyn you might want to buy.

It's a social contract and it's reaffirmed every time a greenback goes from one paw to another.

Put it this way, the US military is behind every buck in Buffett's bank. Every greenback he owns is supported by the most socialistic organization in the American government, the Army.

Now what's all this got to do with anything?

American billionaires haven't amassed their sizable fortunes by themselves. They've worked within the American system of government. They've played it well. They've won the game. If U.S. law had said all computer codes were classified information, Bill Gates would probably be pushing pills for some pharmaceutical conglomerate or other corporate pirate. If Warren Buffett didn't know his way around the tax code, he'd probably be just another nice rich guy. They worked the system as they met it. They knew the rules of the house and they played them.

But now the game isn't working for the vast majority of people playing it. Over the last couple of decades the rules of the game have been changed to screw almost everyone in the United States while at the same time enriching those at the very top of the economic ladder. The rich get to eat bon-bons while the teenage GIs who hold the rifles that protect all the money collect food stamps to feed their own children.

Now those who may have played the game too well cry when anyone suggests changing the rules again. They protest that they made their money all by themselves. They don't see any reason to give those kids holding the guns enough to feed their families. Have the rich become too stupid to keep a hold on what they consider to be their own money? Don't they know that if they give a little they won't lose it all? Haven't they ever heard the Wall Street expression, pigs get fed but hogs get slaughtered?

The American financial system exists because of the will of the American people. The American people decide the rules of the game. It's time to change the rules of the game. It's time to give the wealthiest a haircut and once again spread the wealth.

Too many of the richest among us have become far too stupid.

MONDAY, MARCH 14, 2011

SPRING OFFENSIVE 2011

Where We Are Right Now

Step back. Forget day-to-day trivialities. Forget politics. Step back and take a wider view. As a citizen are you proud of where this nation is and where it is heading?

At present the United States has two illegal, full fledged wars going on in Iraq and Afghanistan. Numerous smaller conflicts are occurring as well. We have military bases in dozens of other countries. Was this union created to be an imperial power?

Over the past few decades great strides have been made to eliminate the racist elements of this country's slave past but at present the income disparity between the wealthiest citizens and the poorest may be as great as it has ever been since the Emancipation Proclamation.

Medical doctors are being executed for practicing their profession.

Corporations have been designated virtual citizens. Whatever that is.

Religious intolerance is now mostly directed at Muslims but Atheists, Jews and Catholics are still within grenade distance.

The President has stated that Americans who torture prisoners are not to be prosecuted, thereby violating the laws of the United States of America and the rest of the world.

Both major political parties are in a race to shift income to the richest members of American society by lowering taxes for the wealthiest while at the same time burdening all other Americans with higher taxes and fees.

Both parties have decided that even though the President has stated that "health care should be a human right", that right should be considered a commodity. When another human right, freedom, is considered a commodity, that condition is called slavery.

Capitalism and the free market are taken as ethical markers even though both have nothing to say regarding the human condition. Neither capitalism nor the free market would demand the feeding of their human chattel if such deprivation meant more black ink.

There have been no prosecutions for the most recent economic collapse even though the crimes are obvious to all.

Teachers are taking to the streets.

Will the unemployable students follow?

Is this the beginning of the Spring Offensive 2011?

FRIDAY, FEBRUARY 18, 2011

OBAMA LOOKS BACK FOR THE MAFIA,

NOT FOR THE TORTURERS

Big news today is the rounding up of Mafia members all the way from the balmy shores of New Jersey to the frequently frozen fens of Boston. The Obama Justice Department decided it was about time they should enforce some of the laws of the United States. Attorney General Holder instructed his department that they should look back and notice some actual crimes probably had been committed and the full force of the Department of Justice descended upon a hundred or so Italian-Americans and their associates.

Isn't it wonderful watching all those bad guys being rounded up and forced to march in the ever so popular perp walks.

Gambling, murder, pension fund plundering, you name it, overweight middle-aged men were suddenly busted for it.

There's pretty good odds not a single one of them confessed to their criminal activities before the Feds called their press conference.

Not one of them copped to having ordered the torture of prisoners. There may or may not be photographs of hooded prisoners having live electric cords attached to their bodies while numerous fat bellies consumed uncounted cannoli.

Why has Attorney General Holder decided that he should stop looking ahead and stop not looking back when it comes to the Mob but keep looking ahead and never looking back when it comes to the self-confessed crimes of George W. Bush? Why has the Obama administration decided torture is no longer a criminal offense but bookmaking still is?

Perhaps the recently arrested capos should confess to ordering their soldiers to waterboard their victims instead of instructing them to break the usual kneecaps.

According to Obama administration precedent, confessing to ordering torture grants the penitent unconditional immunity for themselves and their underlings.

So, let's get this figured out. If you make book in New England, you go to jail. If you dip your fingers into a pension account, you go to jail. But if you order the torture of powerless prisoners under your control, you get to brag about your nefarious deeds in a best selling book and have the President of the United States of America dismiss your crimes against humanity as something less worth investigating than running a whore house in Manhattan.

Illegal gambling - worth prosecuting.

Ordering the torture of prisoners by waterboarding - not worth prosecuting.

President Obama and his underlings have demonstrated the complete contempt they have for the law.

Gumby has shown more backbone than either Obama or Holder.

(Is it surprising that there doesn't appear to be any Mafia activity in Chicago?)

THURSDAY, JANUARY 20, 2011

WHILE YOU WERE SLEEPING

It's been two years, are you awake enough now to open your eyes? Or are you still having your sweet dream about a handsome, wise, young man arising from the Midwest who at long last will fulfill a liberal Democratic vision of government? And bring peace and universal health care to the United States?

There are still prisoners being held at Guantanamo. They are being kept there on the intelligence of the same people who brought us to war in Iraq. We know what was promised would be found in Iraq.

Afghanistan remains a war zone. This has been the Democrats' war for some time now. Congratulations. If you voted for, and still support, Obama, you now own the wars. Go immediately to the bathroom and try to wash some off your hands.

Iraq remains under United States occupation. You keep forgetting about that, don't you?

Charter schools continue to foster segregation. Remember segregation? Where the folks with the money had schools for their kids and those without the money could rot in hell?

Still drilling in the Gulf? You betcha, Barack.

Obama, Democrats and Republican cronies continue to increase military spending. But the budget has to be cut somewhere. How many thieving Democrats will it take to get all the money into the hands of the top two percent of the population? Once again, congratulations to the present administration for passing the cornerstone of the Bush agenda, tax breaks for the wealthiest Americans. It takes a tough Democrat to do exactly what the Republicans want him to do.

Nice work on defunding the Social Security Administration by lowering the percentage of withholding. How eminently Republican.

Cuba provided more aid to Haiti than the United States. And that obscenity continues.

Even after mandating that even more fatally flawed private insurance policies be purchased, the United States will continue to have the most piss poor health system of any industrialized country. With the alleged percentage cap on insurance company profits, one of the best ways for those companies to increase their profit will be to increase the cost of medical expenses across the board. Instead of lowering costs, the Obama for profit system will lead to ever expanding medical expenses since that's the way for insurance companies to make the real money. All you Democrats say DUH!

Admitted torturers continue to run free across the United States because the current President refuses to obey the law and prosecute those who ordered or performed torture. That makes two Presidents in a row who are self-admitted criminals.

How we doing so far?

How does it feel to be in the third term of the Bush presidency?

It's time for you to wake up.

Obama has been a colossal failure if you consider yourself to be a liberal Democrat. Obama has been an incredible president if you are inane enough to vote for Republicans.

Keep supporting Obama. Keep supporting wealth disparity, perpetual war, torture, and a failed for profit health care system which will lead to thousands of needless American deaths.

Or better yet, go back to sleep and wake up in eighteen months and start waving your Obama for President flags again.

People shouldn't call others morons.

MONDAY, JANUARY 3, 2011

from CIRCUS RIDER, a novel history by
Peter Breschard

INTRODUCTORY NOTE

When the original manuscript of CIRCUS RIDER
arrived at our workplace, my staff and I were
decidedly cautious. In the course of an ordinary
week, we encounter numerous historical novels
based upon an author's ancestors and the allegedly
amazing, wonderfully wicked, emotionally engaging
events which may or may not have occurred. Under
usual circumstances, these failures at both history
and fiction are rapidly rejected by our editorial
process.

So, I am sure you are asking, what is the difference
between this volume and the thousands of others
which attempt to illuminate long forgotten historical
events? I shall explain.

Of the prodigious number of painters the United
States has produced since its inception more than

two centuries ago, Gilbert Stuart rises head and shoulders above them all. Not only is Stuart acclaimed for his artistic talents, but many of those he chose as his subjects have escaped time's voracious grasp and managed not to disappear from memory. Their faces are now icons of our nation's history. Portraits of George Washington, Thomas Jefferson and John Adams are among the many images Gilbert Stuart created which will linger forever in the American consciousness.

What do Gilbert Stuart and the rest of early American history have to do with the following pages? In 1808, while plying his trade in Boston, Massachusetts, Stuart was approached to immortalize one half of the most famous duo of entertainers ever to perform in these newly minted, and united, States.

Jean Breschard and his partner, Victor Pépin, were highly acclaimed equestrian performers from the world renowned Paris circus of Monsieur Franconi. As had become circus tradition, Breschard and Pépin, having achieved sufficient recognition and experience under M. Franconi, launched their own troop. After two extraordinarily well received seasons in Spain's capital, Madrid, the Circus of Pépin and Breschard sailed to North America where entertainers of their stature and professionalism never had previously performed.

Stuart's likeness of Breschard remains incomplete, much like his most famous portrait of George Washington (reference any one dollar bill). When this Boston portrait painter presumed there would be some future demand for original oil copies (which he created himself) of any particular painting, he would leave the background unfinished as a detailed setting was unnecessary to facilitate reproductions. One can only suppose that this great American master foresaw an audience for copies of the Breschard portrait which might well have rivaled that for his most popular work, the portrait of the father of these United States, George Washington.

Fortunately, the story of George Washington has not been lost or intentionally mislaid, which is more than can be said for the history of Jean Breschard. What follows in these pages is the story of a great American portrait by America's greatest artist. It is a tale of art, war, pirates, politicians, the new frontier; and all the other ingredients necessary for the stew which was this novel democracy. As well as, of course, the circus.

With considerable trepidation, the editorial board and I have left the ordering of chapters as they were when we originally received the manuscript. The author of this work, not the most loquacious of correspondents, has informed us this arrangement represents the progression in which this history was rediscovered and recreated. Although certain readers might experience a minor dose of literary vertigo as they attempt to follow the non-traditional time line, we hope the clientele of this carnival ride will suffer no severe injuries. Fortunately, with fiction, certain liberties may be taken regarding the ebb and flow of chronicled events. Unfortunately, with history; with reputable history; events are best related as they actually occurred. CIRCUS RIDER being a novel history, we elected to follow the less chosen path.

Gilbert Stuart's portraits immortalize many of America's most notable players. This is the story of one of them, and of how he was lost, and now he is found.

Walter L. White

New York, NY

2010

from CIRCUS RIDER by Peter Breschard

available at www.circusrider.org

WEDNESDAY, DECEMBER 1, 2010

PERPETUAL WAR - THANKS DEMOCRATS AND REPUBLICANS

Do you even think about the wars? After ten years of occupation of one Muslim country or another, do you ever stop to think about just how wrong these military actions are?

With all the whining from both parties about nickels and dimes and new economic theories coming out of liberal or conservative think tanks on a daily basis, does anyone ever talk about how much those predator drones cost as they crash into another home wiping out the families of somebody someone somewhere thinks may be a terrorist?

How much does it cost every time the current president decides to put out a death contract on another United States citizen without benefit of the judicial process?

But you read and listen to the idiots who hour after hour, day after day, week after week, repeat the same theme, endlessly, that the economy is the most important problem of the day.

Sure it's the economy.

After all, your tax dollar probably went to pay for that piece of shrapnel which ripped through the brainpan of another child, as unmindful weaponry wiped out the family of another presumed terrorist.

As recently as two days ago these military minded morons didn't even know who they were negotiating with at the highest level. Yet you stupidly buy their declarations that they know exactly who they are assassinating. And if you dismember innocent children, well, that's that. Bloody, mutilated, innocents. After all, the economy is the most important topic of the day.

You think that if you don't allow the professional gunmen to destroy whatever they wish to destroy, dark foreigners will again attack the homeland. Why don't you simply admit you've become a Nazi? Take a look at yourself. You've allowed the executive branch of this government to wage war, imprison whoever they want, and assassinate Americans at will, without any judicial or legislative review. You've surrendered your rights to your fuhrer out of fear. The leader can kill whoever he thinks is necessary to kill in order to protect the homeland.

And there you have it. The news is composed of the ravings of a photogenic ranter from Alaska, the domestic dramas of foreign royals, and idiots espousing capitalism as if it were part of the constitution, and that's the way you like it.

Ten years. How many deaths are you responsible for? You've been financing this carnage but you feel clean because you are not given the opportunity to witness this bloodbath hourly on the tube.

And now the Democrats say troops will occupy Afghanistan at least until 2014.

Obama had a secret plan to end the war. By now you should recognize it as the same plan Richard Nixon had, keep killing until someone stops you.

Have you had enough of the bloodbath? Have you sucked enough life juice from the necks of Afghanis and Iraqis? Have you returned to sanity following your 9-11 breakdown?

You are killing innocents. You are mindlessly supporting those who protect torturers while bombing children.

It's all on you now.

It's all on us.

It is time to stop the madness.

We are destroying this country while at the same time mindlessly killing thousands half a world away.

It is time we try something else.

It's simple.

Stop relinquishing our rights to the military.

Give peace a chance.

TUESDAY, NOVEMBER 23, 2010

SOMETHING A LITTLE DIFFERENT

Nell Corkin, MINIATURE MINIATURES

http://nell-miniminis.blogspot.com/

Every now and then it's nice to publicize the magnificent work of my bride, Nell Corkin. Small packages, very small packages.

WEDNESDAY, OCTOBER 13, 2010

INQUISITION? YOU'RE WELCOME

When did the heat really come down? Some say it was the Inquisition. Nasty Roman Catholic priests persecuting heretics, Jews, Muslims, and whoever else they felt like putting to the rack. Most folks, when they think of it, believe the Inquisition was born in Spain. How wrong they are.

First they came for the Cathars.

Remember the Crusades? Bunch of Europeans attacking the Middle East? Right? Mostly.

Remember the Albigensian Crusade?

Huh?

You can call the Albigensian Crusade the fifth Crusade if you want. Or number four.

Cathars were a bunch of folks in southern France, northern Italy and northern Spain. If you've ever heard of Occitania (southern France, northern Italy and Spain), you get the idea. The Pope in Rome and the very weak King of France (northern district) decided they wanted to expand. They eyeballed some nice real estate along the Mediterranean coast. Possibly the most civilized part of Europe at the time.

Southern France. Cathars had it going. Trading with Africa and Spain and wherever their boats could sail. Language of their own, culture of their own, religion of their own, had their own culture going on. Cathars also traded with the Muslims a bunch.

Nobody knows much about the Cathars other than where they were. What records remain indicate the Pope and company charged the Cathars with being Christian heretics. Probably the usual went down, troops swooped in from the north and the south and what was a viable culture disappeared. Northern France and the Pope's chunk of Italy ran this Crusade against their neighbors for twenty years.

Cathars were described as being as bad as Muslims are described today. And these were their fellow Europeans. Hell, the Pope and the King used the same play book they published for looting the Holy Land. Get the heretics out of there. Find out who isn't a true believer and put them to sleep. But how do you find out who isn't a true believer when they look like us? So, these Crusaders invented the Inquisition.

Yep. Spain has been getting a bad rap for centuries. The Inquisition was invented in France. During a Crusade against folks now considered Frenchmen. Let France take the heat for the big I. France knows how to take heat like that. The Inquisition was created to ferret out French heretics, or whatever the Cathars actually were. Most all the Cathars were supposedly wiped out, and guess what? Nobody remembers the slaughter of the Cathars, because nobody remembers or knows exactly who the Cathars were. Put it this way, the Inquisition worked on the Cathars. In a way.

Why bring this all up now?

Crusades were easy to think through. Go to the Holy Land and wipe out those pesky Muslims. Muslims, you know they'll start with the Holy Land and then take over everything. What century are we talking about here? Right. The first three or four Crusades. Guess the Muslims gave the Christians too hard a time so the Pope and his pals turned their attention to easier prey.

I can hear them now. Some wise ass surviving Cathar. First they came for the Muslims. Then they came for me. Weren't they supposed to keep massacring the Muslims? Hey, we may be heretics but even the Pope says we're Christian heretics. Not us. See, we've even got Jesus tattoos. This isn't right. You're only supposed to be slaughtering Muslims. Hey, we live on the bloody Riviera!

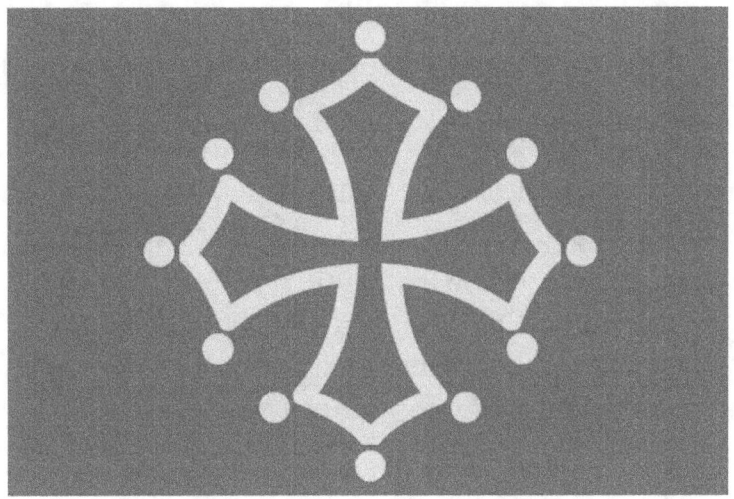

Too bad. The Dominican Order was given the cool job of following the conquering troops into southern France and finding out who all the nasty heretical Cathars were. They asked a lot of questions and the Inquisition was born. The Dominicans did such a great job moving the Cathars completely underground they went looking for other folks who didn't please the Pope. Shalom. Thanks to historians like Mel Brooks and Monty Python, we all have an idea of how the Inquisition progressed after that.

So why the history lesson?

Not the reason you might think.

When the Cathars went underground some think they morphed into other things. The Huguenots. The Quakers. The Shakers. All sorts of interesting little groups, many of whom don't think war is the answer. Hey, that might have been one of the reasons they disappeared when the Crusaders and the Inquisition were wiping everyone out.

Names may have been changed to protect the innocents.

WEDNESDAY, SEPTEMBER 1, 2010

PROTESTANT TERRORISTS TO ERECT CHURCH ACROSS FROM STILL SMOLDERING WHITE HOUSE

August 24, 1815

Hundreds of enraged United States patriots gathered today, across the street from our still smoldering White House, to protest the construction of a proposed Protestant church directly opposite the Presidential Palace, where workmen still labor to rebuild the burned out wreckage.

"It's like shoving a stick in our eye," said Charles O'Madigan, an artisan who lives in the District of Columbia, "exactly one year ago, Protestant troops put the torch to most of our city, and burnt the very home of beloved President and his most illustrious wife. These Protestants building their shrine directly across the avenue from that great house is an insult of the first order."

Such was the majority opinion of those gathered to protest the construction of St. John's Church, at a site they considered far too close to the not yet rebuilt White House. "Those Protestant Red Coats tried to burn our fair city to the ground," opined Jean Beauville, a government employee, "and now their co-religionists are rubbing salt into our wounds. It's just not right. It's just not right I tell you."

The protestors were all but unanimous in the opinion that those erecting the house of worship had a right to do so, however, there was also agreement that building a Protestant shrine this close to where the

White House has yet to be rebuilt was insulting at best.

"Those Protestants are showing poor judgement in the extreme," was the last word on the subject, voiced by Abraham Stuart of Maryland, "they want a memorial to their terrorist attack on our White House. It's just not right."

****

In a related matter, it has been disclosed that Benjamin Latrobe, the architect for the new church, is not a Frenchman as has been popularly assumed. Mr. Latrobe is from Britain. It is believed Mr. Latrobe is also a Protestant.

WEDNESDAY, AUGUST 18, 2010

CHICKEN BY THE BRICK

Read to the end before you begin. Step-by-step directions are overrated.

If you've gotten this far in the book, you're feeling confident by now. You should have some new skills. You are ready for a challenge. Now is the time to get down, dirty, and bloody. It's barbecue (grilling) time. (Not to be confused with real barbecue but that's a whole other item.)

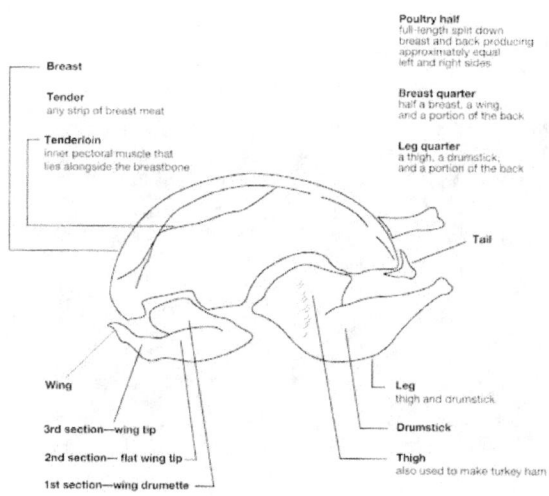

Poultry half
full-length split down breast and back producing approximately equal left and right sides

Breast

Tender
any strip of breast meat

Breast quarter
half a breast, a wing, and a portion of the back

Tenderloin
inner pectoral muscle that lies alongside the breastbone

Leg quarter
a thigh, a drumstick, and a portion of the back

Tail

Wing

Leg
thigh and drumstick

3rd section—wing tip

Drumstick

2nd section— flat wing tip

1st section—wing drumette

Thigh
also used to make turkey ham

Hey, remember that Brick you wrapped in aluminum foil and used to make one hell of a grilled cheese sandwich?

Well, find it. You might still be using it as a handsome door stop or as a Stanley Kubrick action figure, but now's the time to put it to its primary function. Cooking. And in this particular case, outdoor grilling (barbeque?).

Go forth and multiply. You're going to need two bricks for this particular job. So, find another brick. Go ahead. I'll wait.

Waiting.

Waiting.

Waiting.

Mission accomplished. Two bricks at hand. One should already be wrapped in aluminum foil. So wrap the other one so they're twins. Stand back and admire your work.

If you're inside, pick up the silver bricks and take them outside to where you should have an outdoor grill ready and waiting. (If you don't have an outdoor grill, you really didn't need to wrap that extra brick, just peruse the rest of this for the sheer enjoyment.)

Now what I've got is one of those medium size Weber kettle grills. Black. I can almost put my arms around it when it's cool enough. You know what I'm talking about. Making sure you don't inflict massive burns upon yourself should be your primary objective in any cooking exercise. If you don't have similar equipment, modify as you will. I can't think of everything.

Make sure there aren't any dead varmints or rotting plants inside your grill. Fully open the vents. You want that air to flow and your fire to roar. Now take hold of your briquette chimney. Cram the top full of as many briquettes as you can. Take a crumbled sheet of newspaper (or other fiery paper item if you've given up on reading dead tree products), and stuff that into the bottom of your chimney. Don't jam it up too much, leave some room for it to breathe in fire before it transforms into ash.

Take out your handy box or book of matches (no lighters, show a little class), and ignite the newspaper. Stand back and admire your work for a minute or two.

Beer me.

Kill a couple of minutes.

After about five minutes check your chimney and make sure the coals are smoking. Wave your hand a dozen inches above the coals. You should be able to feel the heat. The briquettes should be ready for grilling in about 30 minutes. Most of the briquettes will have turned ashy white.

In the meantime go back inside.

Now for the fun part. You should have had the chicken sitting on your counter for a bit. Taking the chill off.

Unwrap the chicken.

See if they've included gizzards and the like in the cavity of the bird. If they have, take them out and chuck them. A better cook than you or I would know what to do with this stuff, but you'll have to communicate with them if you want to find out.

Toss the bird on a cutting board near the sink.

Find the bird's backbone.

From here on in it's going to get sloppy and messy. What could be more fun?

What you want to do here is separate the bird's spine from the rest of the carcass. You can do this with a sharp knife, boning is good, but it might have been a good idea to previously have invested in a pair of poultry shears. (Pair? Collective nounism at its finest.)

Get that spine out of there. (Now it will truly be chicken.)

Flatten the bird with skin side down. You should be looking at the breast bones.

Get rid of them. Shears, knives, fingers. Greasy. Sloppy. Innards. Cool.

Once you've detached that breast bone (Very little description here, you have to have the experience yourself.), spread that bird out on the board. It's called butterflying. You're turning what was a three dimensional object into something that more closely resembles a two dimensional object. Give or take an inch, verging on the infinite.

Might not be a bad time to rinse the bird, then use some paper towels to pat it dry.

Use a brush or another paper towel to spread some vegetable oil all over both sides of the 2D poultry.

Now if you've been paying attention and pre-read these instructions, you should have already combined the salt, pepper, cumin, garlic powder and cayenne pepper.

Rub this tasty combo into both sides the bird. There should be a healthy amount left over.

Wash your hands.

Check the time. If its around half an hour since you started the coals go out and take a look. If not kill some time. Beer me.

When the briquettes are right, spread them out on the bottom of the grill. I usually dump them into one half, the hot side, and leave the other side alone. Up to you. Make sure the cooking surface is in place.

Almost forgot, I like to use is a black flat metal sheet with punched holes in it which is used for grilling fish and the like. You need a flat piece of metal, preferably with holes. You figure it out. Your choice. Have it near the grill.

Grab the chicken and head out to the grill.

Toss the bird onto the hot side. Skin side down. Cover the bird with the aerated sheet of metal. Put your two bricks on top of the sheet. Put the cover on top of the grill.

Set your timer for thirteen minutes.

Beer me.

After 13 put on your gloves. Open the grill. Grab a brick. Toss the very hot brick between your hands until you find a safe place to put it. Concrete and fireproof is usually smart. Do the same with the other brick. Grab the metal sheet and put it on top of the bricks.

Use your tongs to flip the chicken.

Replace the metal sheet and bricks then put the cover on the grill. Set the time for 14 minutes.

Beer me.

After 14 close the vents on your grill. Vacate everything and take the now great tasting bird to wherever you intend to dine.

Cover the bird loosely with aluminum foil and let it sit for eight minutes.

After you and whoever have consumed this bird, you will be proclaimed king by acclamation.

Beer me.

what you're going to need

one whole chicken (you usually get what you pay for)

poultry shears (say what?)

outdoor grill

briquettes

briquette chimney

matches

newspaper

cutting board

sharp knives

running water

paper towels

aluminum foil

measuring spoons

1 ½ tablespoon large grain sea salt

2 teaspoon freshly ground black pepper

1 teaspoon whole cumin, toasted and ground

2 teaspoons garlic powder

3/4 teaspoon cayenne

cooking oil

flat piece of metal preferably with holes and big
enough to cover a chicken

2 bricks wrapped in aluminum foil

heavy leather work gloves (heat resistant)

tongs

plates, knives, forks, napkins

timer

beer

TUESDAY, AUGUST 3, 2010

THE FIRST AMERICAN CIRCUS

John Bill Ricketts introduced the modern circus to the United States in 1793. His first North American shows were in Philadelphia, Pennsylvania, where, among others, he entertained George Washington. Everyone's best guess is that Ricketts was either an Englishman or a Scot. There is some debate regarding his nation of origin. John Bill Ricketts never settled in America and was last reported sailing away to either Europe or the Caribbean in 1799.

In 1807, embarking from Madrid, Victor Pepin and Jean Baptiste Breschard brought their circus to the Commonwealth of Massachusetts (sometimes recognized as being part of the United States). Breschard was a Frenchman and Pepin was born in the Empire State, New York.

Ricketts' Circus and The Circus of Pepin and Breschard were the first two major circus companies to play in North America, specifically in what had recently become the United States of America.

This November PBS will dedicate six hours of national broadcasting to their documentary, CIRCUS. Undoubtedly, some questions regarding the origins of the circus in the United States will be raised.

(Disclaimer: similarities in name between this article's author and any mentioned subject are duly noted.)

Over the years, John Bill Ricketts has been described by many writers, many times, as operating and headlining the first American circus.

"The first American circus?" What do they mean by that?

Is there an "American" style circus which was created by Ricketts?

No, they're not talking about an American style of circus. The modern circus, of which John Bill's company was a fine example, is as European as it gets.

Was John Bill an American who ran a circus?

Nope. (See above.)

What circus historians (say what?) have been trying to say for years isn't that John Bill Ricketts ran the first American circus. What they've been trying to say is that JBR operated the first circus in America (specifically within the U.S.A.).

When Enrico Caruso performed in the United States, he didn't become an American tenor. Ricketts' Circus remained a British circus performing in America just like Enrico remained an Italian tenor even though he might have been belting it out within the continental U.S. at the time..

Now who exactly is responsible for the first American circus? (Have I already tipped my hand?)

Since it has been established that there is no particular American style of circus (rodeo?), the first circus operated by (owned and starring) an American (U.S.A.) would probably be "the first American circus".

Hello, Victor Pepin.

What's led to a bit of confusion among circus historians is that the Circus of Pepin and Breschard is documented as having played in Madrid, Spain, immediately before its arrival in the Bay State. Circus historians have referred to P & B's troupe as being a French circus, a Spanish circus, and a European company. My guess is that it has been perhaps too hard for all-American writers to realize that a guy with a French surname (Pepin) could have been a creator of the first American circus.

The Circus of Pepin and Breschard - The First American Circus

Anybody want some Freedom Fries?

TUESDAY, JULY 20, 2010

AMERICANS ON THE AUCTION BLOCK

If health care is a human right as is avowed by most industrial countries, what can be said of those corporations and human beings who profit from the current health care system in the United States which treats health care as a commodity?

Can anyone ethically treat a human right as a commodity?

Can any human being ethically promote unnecessary shortages of medical necessities in order to manipulate the price of said medical necessities?

Are corporations, legally compelled to create the greatest profit for shareholders, designed to increase the pain and suffering of human beings in order to increase demand for product and inflate profit margins?

If health care is a human right equivalent to liberty, how can individual health care be put on the auction block?

Let's try it this way. Say the 2010 Liberty Bill provided that each citizen in the United States needed to be covered by liberty insurance to be provided by their employer or purchased individually. The bill calls for some governmental assistance for most citizens who are unable to purchase policies for themselves, however, even under the rosiest of scenarios 24,000 Americans will be unable to obtain full coverage, and so will be deprived of their liberty.

Prior to the American Civil War, auctions used to be held for human beings who were unfortunate enough not to carry liberty insurance.

Even for those who admit that health care is a human right similar to liberty, there appear to be few willing to follow this thought to its logical conclusion.

Prior to the abolition of slavery in this country, there were individuals and companies involved in the slave trade and directly in the exploitation of slave labor. Companies and individuals profiting from the deprivation of another person's human rights, how was that different from the situation today? Are not the health insurance companies profiting from the denial of universal health care to United States citizens? Is this not the equivalent of putting today's Americans on the auction block and those who have the wherewithal to purchase their freedom from disease and illness will keep their health while those who cannot will be denied what is almost universally recognized as a human right, health care.

Are we willing to consider people and companies who profit directly from the buying and selling of the human right of health care in the same light we consider those who buy and sell slaves? Are we willing to realize that every dime paid into health insurance companies is a dime which will be used to promote the practice of denying human rights to Americans?

Are we willing to realize that mealy mouthed politicians who proclaim that health care should be a right for every American, don't realize that rights either are or aren't. If health care should be a right, then it obviously isn't one now. Any politician who isn't for universal health care is condemning those not covered to the deprivation of a human right. The 2010 health care bill condemned at least 24,000 Americans a year to such deprivation of human rights.

It's time to start considering health insurance companies the same way you consider slavers. It's time to start considering those government officials who are not actively seeking universal health care the same way you view those politicians who actively supported slavery. It's time to ostracize those members of the community who actively support or trade in the present system of for profit health care and the insurance companies that profit from the ills of Americans.

Some say the United States system of health care is the best in the world. Some used to say the United States system of cotton delivery was the best in the world. When something's wrong, it's wrong.

FRIDAY, JULY 16, 2010

WHEN CORPORATIONS ATTACK

(A ROUGH RANT)

Now that we've all noticed how much we're bleeding, you might want to take a look to see what is causing all the damage.

Let's see, what's been happening lately? Afghanistan has become the longest running war ever waged by the United States. Oil is killing much of the life in and around the Gulf of Mexico. A good portion of America's wealth has disappeared from what was once known as Wall Street.

Now what do all these wonderful events have in common?

In case you haven't noticed, CORPORATIONS HAVE DECLARED WAR ON THE UNITED STATES.

BP is currently destroying the ecology and the economy of the Gulf Coast.

Every weapon manufacturer and two-bit service company in the world is bankrupting the US by scamming every buck we can print from the wars in Iraq and Afghanistan.

What was left of the US budget after the Iraq and Afghanistan scams was diverted to the international banks when they threatened to bring Europe and North America back into the Great Depression.

If a bunch of fundamentalist idiots flying airplanes did half the damage to the US as BP has already done, the United States would have attacked England without even passing a declaration of war.

It's time to get with the concept, corporations are out to destroy everything which the United States has stood for all these years. Corporations are programmed to be killing machines and now they have turned against us. What controls the people of the United States once possessed have been discarded or ignored.

Wake up!!! We are under attack by an enemy who has already subverted a majority of the population. Most workers put their current paychecks before everything else.

And let's not forget the thousands of American citizens who will die each and every year because the insurance corporations and bankers, and the politicians who work for them refused to allow any form of universal health care to become law in this land.

Start counting the bodies. How many thousands of civilians have given up their lives in Iraq and Afghanistan in what are entirely corporate wars? How many US military gunmen and mercenaries along with the "enemy" combatants in those two countries have died so companies like Halliburton can pay a higher dividend?

Corporations have also attacked our food supply, giving us frankenfoods which contribute to the bottom line of numerous corporations while also contributing to the corporate health care system currently in place. Corporate animal factories may soon become lethal beyond description. The health benefits of bio-diversity inherently conflict with the ideals of mass production and distribution.

Put them all together. What do all of these for-profit corporations have in common? Why do for-profit corporations exist? For-profit corporations exist only to make money. These corporations do not give a rat's ass about human beings. They don't support any form of government. For-profit corporations exist for only one purpose, to grind every possible penny out of whatever they control. Anything that gets in the way of corporate profit is to be either bought off or destroyed.

How did this happen? Multi-national corporations is one of the answers. Generations back, even if those who truly owned the corporations couldn't be touched, the senior management could be somewhat swayed by public opinion. These human beings had to live in communities where pressure could be exerted to keep some minimal form of social control. But now corporate higher ups can be transferred from jurisdiction to jurisdiction at jet speed. And those corporate officers who need to stay in a single jurisdiction usually end up in gated communities surrounded by similar multi-national fugitives. They no longer have the need to interact with society in general. Laws and mores of individual countries mean nothing to these organizations. Quarterly returns are their gods and civilizations.

Maximizing shareholders' returns doesn't mean being a good citizen. It means what it says.

Anthropomorphizing isn't just what Disney does to the animal kingdom. Anthropomorphizing is what the corporate media does every day as they try to portray what are basically computer programs, corporations, as having human emotions. Corporations don't feel anything. Corporations aren't a "they". For-profit corporations are contracts designed to maximize profit. Corporations are greed on paper and in the legal system.

What has happened is the US has entirely lost regulatory control of the business community. It's as if the Air Force were deciding what missions it wished to undertake. Anyone who believes that left unfettered the for-profit corporate community would not bring back slavery is a fool. Why wouldn't it?

Enough for now.

WEDNESDAY, JUNE 16, 2010

OBAMA SAYS:

OFFSHORE DRILLING IS COOL!

Obama doesn't spill, he uses a napkin.

Isn't he just the most wonderful Democrat you could possibly imagine!

At least Bush didn't promote the flooding of US cities.

TUESDAY, MAY 4, 2010

BREAD/CHEESE/BRICK

Let's all ruminate upon the simple brick.

Clay and water. Fired.

Pavers of our streets. Mainstays of our walls. Enablers of our shithouses.

Fashion statement for student bookshelves.

Rioter's friend.

What gets laid more?

But like everything that active, bricks need protection.

First, put your hands on a brick. Regular size (8" x 4" x 2 1/4", if you want stats) , nothing fancy. Red, if available.

Second; wrap-up said building supply in aluminum foil. (Why do we need the brick to be red? Ask a fireman wearing colorful suspenders.)

Easily at hand should be; frying pan (any), butter (real), bread (good), yellow cheese (sliced), yellow mustard (or mustardy mustard, Colonel).

Now you're getting the idea.

Fire up that spacious flat thing in your kitchen called the cooktop (burners). It's usually right above your stove and powered by electricity or some sort of gas. (See chapter, Survival on Big Blue, if you're having any trouble up to this point.)

Place frying pan on heat source, medium high heat.

Butter. If the butter is warm, like room temperature, spread this cow product on one side of two pieces of bread. Or to be more specific, spread butter on one side of each slice of bread. If butter is colder, cut off around 1/2 inch from stick (assumed) and toss into warming frying pan. Now how hard was that?

Spread some mustard on the unbuttered sides of bread, or on either side if bread previously unbuttered.

Next, grab a couple of slices of cheese and carefully place between two mustardy sides of bread. Remember: you want both the mustard and the cheese to be situated between the two slices of bread and the unbuttered/unmustarded or buttered/unmustarded sides to be on the outside.

By now the frying pan should be nice and hot and the butter in the pan, if butter is in the pan, should be making a little noise. Spread the butter around a bit with the bread/cheese/mustard concoction you've just made.

Place the bread/cheese/mustard in the frying pan.

Pick up your aluminum foil wrapped brick and gently place it on top of the bread in the pan. Press down a little. Not too much.

Wait a minute or two, depending upon the heat of the pan, until you start to smell burning bread.

Take off the brick, set on a different burner on your cooktop, and using a spatula or knife, lift up your sandwich and see if it toasted to a color which suits your appetite. (You won't get this right for a bit, but you'll eventually figure it all out.)

If it looks right to you, it is right.

Flip it over in the pan.

Put brick back on.

Wait a minute or two. Remove brick. Cheese should have melted some by this time.

Turn off burner.

Remove sandwich from pan.

Let cool a bit.

Eat.

You are now king in the land of the blind.

Additional uses for aluminum enshrouded brick when not being used as a gourmet aid; doorstop, hatholder, Stanley Kubrick tribute, paperweight, mail minder, action figure pedestal.

SATURDAY, APRIL 24, 2010

NO SEX FOR DEMOCRATS

After nearly a year-and-a-half of Republicans taking control of the Democratic Party, it's time for the referees to start calling fouls. After Barack Obama has shown he can hustle more private insurance policies than anyone could ever have imagined and peddle infinitely more patent medicine than any fever dreamed snake oil salesman, it is time to blow the whistle on the Obama brand of corporate Republicanism.

A quick reminder. Doubling the number of troops in Afghanistan under Obama. How many troops are in Iraq right now? (Comparing anyone to George W. Bush should be the definition of damning by faint praise.) Obama's refusal to prosecute torturers. (A crime in itself.) Predator drone assassinations. Shoveling trillions to Wall Street. (Tax breaks for small business? What Republican in the past

129

hundred years hasn't campaigned on that canard?) Passing a Health Care Bill weaker than that introduced by Republican Bob Dole over sixteen years ago. How many times does Obama have to prove to us that he really is a corporate Republican?

Forget Obama. It's time to go Lysistrata on the entire Democratic Party.

Now let's not get all in a lin tizzy about this. We all know that politicians are a sexless bunch of power junkies who wouldn't be at all phased by withdrawal of intimate human contact. Pols only care about one thing, votes. It's time to pull out of the Democratic Party until they promise to come across with something worthy of our affections.

This year, if your Democratic senator, congressman, governor, dog catcher, whatever does not support Medicare for All Americans, and does not pledge to help introduce legislation to that effect, cross your legs, withdraw your essence, and let them know your vote is going elsewhere. Vote Green if you want. Write in if you feel like it. (The correct spelling of my name should be at the top of this article.) Stop supporting the corporate Democratic/Republican party. And make sure you let them know why they've lost your support. It is time to act. There is a national election coming up in a few months. Obama and his Democrats have proven that they would rather sell private insurance company policies than campaign for universal health care. Now is the time to pull out of the Democrat Party until they come across.

LYSISTRATA.

It's game time. How many more American will die because corporations are allowed to run health care?

SATURDAY, APRIL 3, 2010

REFUSE TO VOTE FOR ANY DEMOCRAT WHO ISN'T 100% BEHIND MEDICARE FOR ALL AMERICANS.

MAKE SURE YOU LET THEM KNOW WHY AND WHERE YOUR VOTE IS GOING

THE LETHAL DOWNSIDE
TO THE HEALTH
REFORM BILL

By not attempting to pass any form of universal health care, President Obama has helped condemn 23,000 Americans a year to unnecessary deaths.

How did this lethal equation come into being?

Why was Single Payer never pushed by the White House?

Why was the Public Option given the most meager of lip service by Obama?

Who decided 23,000 deaths a year was acceptable collateral damage?

Did anyone ever actually say, "Mr. President, if you don't push for universal coverage, we can get this through and you won't expend any of your political capital. Only 23,000 Americans will die every year, but that's OK with us."

Why aren't more people discussing the deals made by the White House with the pharmaceutical companies and the hospitals? Did these deals have anything to do with the White House not campaigning for Single Payer or universal health care? Have these deals ever been published on the Web or anywhere else? Or were these the ultimate backroom arrangements which will leave 23,000 Americans a year to die?

Transparency in this White House? I think not.

The argument used is that this pitiful health care reform bill was the best they could do. I'm not going to get into why that is a laughable defense, but we all know, you can't win if you don't try. The White House didn't try. Never once did Obama use his bully pulpit to demand that 23,000 Americans not die each year.

23,000 living Americans are just a bit more important than "bending the cost curve."

Today 23,000 Americans a year will be allowed to die unnecessary deaths. That's less than it would have been without this present bill but it is the least that could have been done. It is a meager achievement at best and a massive sales job by the insurance companies at worst.

Today 23,000 Americans a year might have been saved if President Obama had raised his voice in righteous indignation and demanded that the right to health care be enforced in this country.

But instead Obama did nothing to save them.

Obama and all those in government who did not use the power of their positions to demand universal health care, have chosen to allow 23,000 Americans a year to die unnecessarily.

For someone known for his oratory, President Obama kept surprisingly silent as 23,000 Americans a year were left to die.

Congratulations on passing your bill.

SUNDAY, MARCH 21, 2010

GREED NEEDS A SIN TAX

It doesn't matter if the wealthiest 5% of the people in this country control 70, 80, or 90% of this country's wealth. It doesn't matter if they pay more taxes at a slightly higher rate. What matters is how you define greed.

Sin taxes are governmental levies on perceived evil substances such as tobacco and alcohol. People feel comfortable hitting those products with extra taxes because, hey, we all know booze and tobacco are bad for you. We're just helping you out by making these products more expensive to buy. It's called negative reinforcement. If you smoke or drink, it's going to hurt you in the pocketbook when you buy them.

Not only do tobacco and alcohol hurt you, they also harm those who come into contact with smokers and boozers.

Isn't greed something society should help its citizens overcome? Not only is greed bad for the individual, but greed harms society as well.

Greed is one of the seven deadly sins.

Ask any good Bible reading Christian. Greed is bad. Greed is a sin.

Let's tax greed. If we don't tax greed, we might as well not tax tobacco and liquor. Smoking and drinking don't even make it onto the top seven sin list. Greed is not good.

Back in the glory days of the 50s and even during the mythic days of the Gipper, the top tax rate on income was something close to twice what it is today. Somehow the rich stayed rich but surprisingly, the poor did not get poorer. The gap between the rich and the rest of the citizenry was a whole lot less than it is today. There was still greed, but it wasn't as rewarded as it is today. Greed was taxed, seriously. And somehow this country and its people prospered.

The more you tax high incomes, the more trivial high incomes become.

It's time to bring back the 70% top federal tax bracket. This would do wonders for the federal budget and, besides, it's the Christian thing to do. Helping our fellow man avoid the sin of greed is probably a spiritual work of mercy.

It's time to seriously tax the extemely rich. Greed isn't good for any of us.

THURSDAY, MARCH 11, 2010

SO TAX ME FOR LIVING

If you live and breathe in the United States you are about to be taxed. Not your income. Not your property. You are about to be taxed simply for living. And breathing. You are about to be charged a fee for your right to life in the United States of America. Welcome to the Breath Tax.

(Disclaimer: Opening up Medicare for all Americans is the only moral and efficient way to deal with the present healthcare situation. Imagine how much money would be saved by putting the private insurance pencil pushers out to pasture.)

Think about it for a second. Forcing every American, under penalty of law, who is not covered by public insurance to be covered by private insurance is possibly the most egregious tax ever levied upon the citizens of these United States. This unprecedented transfer of private funds into the coffers of corporations is the harbinger of the coming of a corporate state.

What Obama's Democrats are proposing is the equivalent of a tax for living. Never before has any American been taxed simply for breathing. And to add insult to injury, the money will not be going into Federal coffers, it will end up in the pockets of insurance companies, enabling them to finance even more campaigns aimed at extorting even greater sums from Americans.

You breathe, you pay a private insurance company, unless you're already under Federal protection. Your money or your life. I wouldn't feel so bad about all of this if at least there were a public option where my money would not be used by private companies who would rather see me die than take away money from their shareholders. At least the Federal government isn't bound to increase earnings for stock holders. It's bad enough being taxed to breathe, but to pay the money to corporations, who by law do not have your best interests at heart, well, that's a little hard to take.

The Breath Tax, certainly has a ring to it doesn't it? Unless you are over 65, disabled, a veteran, a child, you are going to be forced to pay money to private insurance companies, either indirectly, through your employer, or out of your own pocket.

I hate to bring this up, but Obama's Breath Tax is a poll tax.

Remember the old poll taxes? Poll taxes were used to keep minorities from voting. Obama's breath tax isn't exactly that.

A poll tax is a capitation tax. Poll used to mean "head." What we're talking about here is counting heads which is what happens when you go to the polls and vote. No doubt this is a bit confusing but there you have it. The trick is that the US doesn't use poll taxes. Hasn't in quite some time. A poll tax is a regressive tax if there ever were one. In other words, Bill Gates and anybody pulling in 40 grand a year are subject to the same minimum tariff. The same minimum tariff to be paid to some insurance company represented by Joe Lieberman.

So there you have some information. The Breath Tax demands you pay money to corporate insurers. Obama's Breath Tax puts tax money directly into private hands. Today's Democrats are presenting no other option.

There's only one way to avoid the Obama Breath Tax.

MONDAY, MARCH 1, 2010

OBAMA, SLAVERY, AND HEALTH CARE

President Obama - The Member from South Carolina will be recognized.

Congressman Blowhard - Thank-you, Mr. President. As has been previously discussed, the report from the Congressional Budget Office clearly indicates that freeing any of the Slaves currently held in bondage within these United States will result in ongoing deficits for at least the next decade. I think we can all agree on this.

Vice-President Biden - We have to reduce the cost curve.

Senator Lame - The people of the United States have clearly indicated their preference. They don't want any change to the current law. They know that freeing any of the current slaves into the work force will reduce their wages.

President Obama - Now I think we have more areas of agreement here than disagreement. That's why I'm currently proposing that instead of freeing all of the slaves at this point in time, we come to an agreement that current slave holders should be allowed to purchase as many slaves as possible for the next four years and that all current slaves should at some time in the future be allowed the right to purchase their own freedom through federal exchanges which will negotiate a better price than that which individual slaves would be capable of negotiating themselves.

Congressman Blowhard - What we need are state exchanges which will negotiate under current existing law.

Vice-President Biden - What we all agree upon here is that these slaves are a commodity. I think we can all agree that human life is a commodity? Can we not?

President Obama - Joe, you're exactly right there. After all, what is human life and well being other than a commodity which at the moment is way out of whack with what this country needs right now.

We're here to figure out how to keep the cost of this commodity to a minimum.

Senator Lame - What we don't want here is the Federal Government setting the price for our slaves. Individual States know what's best for their own people. I agree we have to keep the price of this commodity down, but Federal interference is nowhere in the Constitution.

President Obama - I think we can all agree that human beings are a commodity and the price curve should be brought down. Let's talk some more.

THURSDAY, FEBRUARY 25, 2010

SHOULD OBAMA RESIGN TODAY?

Should President Obama resign?

Today?

Yesterday?

Tomorrow?

You can mark me down as being in the Tomorrow column. Yesterday or Today are a bit too unreasonable for me.

I know Obama being in office for another twenty-four hours means another one hundred and twenty-three people have died unnecessarily because they lack health insurance, but I think the gentleman from Chicago should be given the time to neatly pack his belongings and leave. Having him rush out of town as if an angry mob were after him is not justified. Resigning by tomorrow will be fine with me.

What did we expect? Barack Obama had the least pertinent experience of any elected President in the past hundred years. (If you want to say W was even worse that's fine. Just remember you're the one comparing Obama to Bush. I pray Obama is incompetent rather than corrupt.)

Everyone was enamored by the young, good looking, intelligent legislator from the Land of Lincoln . Barack was so much better than George.

Get over it.

Obama is a horrible president. Almost as bad as Bush.

It's time for Obama to resign.

He's unfit for the job.

(Abetting torture by not prosecuting torturers. Doubling troops in Afghanistan. Predator drone assassinations. Useless on Health Care Reform., etc.)

SATURDAY, FEBRUARY 20, 2010

22,500 DEMOCRATIC DEATHS AND COUNTING

If 45,000 Americans die each year because they are uninsured, how many of these deaths are now the responsibility of the Democratic Party? Since gaining control of the legislative and executive branches fourteen months ago, the Democrats under Obama have accomplished nothing in stopping these unnecessary deaths. Even giving them eight months to get their act together (Obama's August 2009 target date), they now have six months of responsibility for uninsured deaths on their hands. That's 22,500 preventable deaths. And counting.

In a similar vein.

Artists die young.

Why?

Let's face it, the way this country rewards or punishes behaviors is through the tax code and other financial programs. You can get thousands back from your government if you purchase a certain type of gas guzzler. You can write off from your taxes what you spend on sporting events. (If you are properly incorporated.) You get reimbursed for not growing crops. You can receive reimbursement for college tuition if you're willing to be employed as a gunman/woman for a few years.

When I read this eulogy, I remembered my friend, Helen. Helen died because she couldn't figure out how to be an artist and maintain proper health care. She was presented with the choice, work as an artist or stop being the artist she was and waste her energy on jobs where she worked only to be able to afford health insurance. She chose to be an artist. She carried useless health insurance. And so she died.

Shows you how much this country values human life and original thought.

That would be not at all.

And now the responsibility lies in the hands of the Democratic Party. 22,500 so far.

Hey, Olberman! You've been harping on the number of days since Bush declared victory in Iraq for years now. I'm not saying you should stop. But lets add a number to your daily routine. March 1, 2010 will be six full months since August 2009.

Number of Preventable Deaths since President Obama said we should have a Health Care reform bill passed.

22,500

And then add 123 more each and every day until Obama's Democratic Party acts humanely.

22,623

22,746

22,869

22,992

etc.

etc.

MONDAY, FEBRUARY 22, 2010

YOUR MONEY OR YOUR LIFE, DR. LIME

One of my all time favorite movies is The Third Man, directed by Carol Reed. When Graham Greene adapted his novella into a screenplay, perhaps the world was a more understandable place. The post World War II period never seemed simple to me. Somehow I doubt life was any less complicated back then, but that's nostalgia for you.

Poor Holly Martins (Joseph Cotton) arrives in multi-occupied Vienna after being offered work by his friend, Harry Lime (Orson Welles). Martins soon discovers that Lime has been run over by the proverbial bus (lorry) and will not soon be delivering on any promised employment.

Moving right along, Martins discovers that Harry Lime was a black marketeer of the most nefarious type. Lime stole a shipment of penicillin and, after watering it down, sold it back to the medical community. Unfortunately the diluted penicillin is possibly worse than worthless and numerous children have allegedly either died or been crippled by Lime's product.

Harry Lime is portrayed as the most despicable of

human beings. A cretinous bug. But this was all back in the 1950s when things were simpler. Back then a scumbag was a scumbag, even if you couldn't use the word scumbag in polite society.

Harry Lime, the lowest of the low, profiteer and thief.

But let's hold on a second. That was how hateful Harry was perceived sixty years ago. Let's have another look at Harry from today's enlightened corporate perspective.

Was Harry ever convicted of a crime? Absolutely not. Allegations he had stolen penicillin were never proven. Innocent until proven guilty.

Did Harry Lime steal the drugs he was accused of reselling? Again, how Harry came into possession of his product has never been adjudicated.

What was Harry Lime's crime? Multiple jurisdictions, no conviction.

What crime? Harry Lime simply maximized profit with the product he had at hand.

Penicillin was a desirable commodity at that time in Vienna. Lime was in possession of a source for the drug and doctors and hospitals were willing to purchase this commodity at venues considered illegal. Certainly the medical community didn't have to make these questionable purchases. These medical professionals chose to buy black market drugs. How could they imagine these illegal drugs would be of the same quality and potency as those obtained through legitimate channels? These medicines should have been tested for quality before they were used on unsuspecting children. Obviously, the medical profession was negligent.

So there you have it. Harry Lime wasn't guilty of anything. All he did was profit on the ill health of those who could afford to pay for his watered down pharmaceuticals.

Today Harry Lime, profiteer and murderer, could easily become an executive for any of numerous American health care providers or drug companies. The Third Man certainly knew how to turn the ill health of innocents into a commodity. Isn't that what it's all about?

Harry Lime, corporate medicine at its finest!

SATURDAY, FEBRUARY 13, 2010

MOVEON, NOTHING HAPPENING HERE, JUST MOVEON

Today I found in my overflowing inbox another email from Moveon.org. I guess I've been on their mailing list for a long time now.

Moveon began with simple goals. Stop talking about your neighbor's sex life. Stop the war in Iraq, get Bush out of office, etc. In general it's a fine organization meant to appeal to the best in us. Stop unnecessary killing and all torture. Things like that.

Moveon helped organize tens of thousands, at least, of young people to get the Democrats in control of the government.

But today's missive was something else again.

Today I was informed that Moveon was now involved with regulating Wall Street. Perhaps they have been doing this for some time. Maybe I previously had just failed to notice. Today I was told that I should send money to Moveon so they could deal with all the criminals involved in the AIG shell game.

Wow! Somebody has discovered there are a bunch of thieves involved in the financial markets!

Now I certainly applaud anyone who has figured out how to deal with the infinite machinations included within our present financial system. And after I introduce you to them, I have a small bridge I can sell to you in Breukelyn. Moveon has just joined the most disreputable of all social beings, the economic pundits. To say this is a comedown is putting it mildly.

Listen! All of you liberal rabble rousers out there, stick with what you know. I seriously do not want Amnesty International telling me how to clean up the environment. I don't want Greenpeace asking me for money to campaign for more libraries. Stick with what you are Moveon.org. Do not pretend to be the financial police. And most certainly don't ask me for money to do something you really shouldn't be doing. Isn't that what got AIG into trouble in the first place?

MONDAY, FEBRUARY 8, 2010

WHY HEALTH INSURANCE COMPANIES LOVE OBAMA

Let's face it, Obama's heart was never with health care reform. He has invested approximately zero of his political capital in creating a new health care insurance system. Zero. Nada. Zilch. For the past year, platitudes have been the only words to escape his lips while he vocally supports not a single specific program.

Democratic Presidents, ex-officio leaders of the Democratic Party, are meant to push specific programs. When Obama was first elected he had tremendous political capital and grassroots support. Over the last year he has frittered away all that momentum. Who can get behind the health care bill of President Platitude? There is no bill. Over the past week Obama has mentioned his health care program on numerous occasions. But there is no such program. He stands for nothing. Obama can speak endlessly about generalities. Perhaps he missed his calling. Perhaps he should be penning greeting cards. "Hope!"

Now who benefits from all this? Obama's opponent in the Democratic primary was Hillary Clinton. If anyone scared the health insurance industry more than Senator Clinton, please let me know. What the health insurance industry needed was a Democratic candidate who could mouth all the right platitudes but who had no particular desire to upset the health insurance industry as it exists today.

All I know is, that after a year, President Platitude has accomplished nothing as far as reforming the health insurance industry is concerned. The insurance companies couldn't have asked for anything more.

FRIDAY, JANUARY 29, 2010

FROM THE MESSAGE BOARD

As posted to the Circus History Message Board

Among the earliest of photographic portraits of circus people are several images of animal presenter Jacob Driesbach. A long-time collector that owned one of them saw fit to bestow an identification of Isaac A. Van Amburgh upon it, having no knowledge of the actual sitter other than his general notoriety. There is no evidence at hand to confirm that Van Amburgh ever sat for a photographer.

The late Stuart Thayer had descriptions of both Driesbach and Van Amburgh. He even found a newspaper reference for the session when and where Driesbach was photographed. Thayer advanced a strong case for his Driesbach identification. Despite overwhelming evidence, others interested in photographic materials refused to accept his findings for fear of alienating the collector.

Thus, the earliest prominent portrait of an American circus owner, as well as some of the earliest photographic portraits of a circus performer are both challenged in their identification. Even with a sound argument at hand, it is often impossible to alter an entrenched mentality until a generational change takes place. Truth falls victim to allegiance, for a variety of reasons, especially in the public eye. Good luck with your establishment of the Breschard identity for the Gilbert Stuart portrait.

Fred Dahlinger

http://www.circushistory.org/Query.htm#3227

Fred Dahlinger is an extremely well respected circus historian.

Generational change does not necessarily need move at a glacial pace.

WEDNESDAY, JANUARY 27, 2010

OBAMA RESIGNS

AP 01-21-10 10:35 PM

In a fit of rampant bi-partisanship, Barack Obama announced today that, "I intend to become the first President (not about to be impeached), the first Black President, the first Hawaiian President, of these United States, to resign from office."

Realizing, at long last, that after one year in the White House his only remaining supporters were paid employees of the war/medical/pharmaceutical/insurance/money laundering machines, today President Obama finally made a proposal upon which both sides of the aisle could agree.

"I mean, seriously folks, why on earth did you ever expect someone with as little experience with the top levels of government to be anything other than a poster boy for military industrial complex? They've been at this for a long, long time. I was in the Senate for what, a couple of weekends? Truly, I am sorry.

The accommodations were wonderful and Michelle and the girls had a great time, but we are so out of here. To tell the truth, I'd rather be on the beaches of the great state of Hawaii."

News of Obama's resignation was greeted with relief. "Joe Biden's no great shakes but at least he isn't going to listen to anything the Republicans have to say." said a senior Senator. This seemed to be the general consensus of most Democrats on hearing the news.

From the other side of the aisle, former Presidential candidate John McCain wished his one time opponent well and "Thank God Barack is doing this. He scared the hell out of us. I mean, was he sleepwalking or what?"

Reached for comment the President presumptive, Vice-President Joe Biden, mentioned something about trains not being available for the additional commute.

THURSDAY, JANUARY 21, 2010

INSCRIPTIONS ON BRESCHARD, THE CIRCUS RIDER, NOT BY GILBERT STUART

There appears to be a good deal of confusion about the two inscriptions at the bottom corners of this painting. As has been shown by the National Gallery of Art, these two inscriptions were placed on the canvas years after the work was completed. The guesses as to what the names may be are both many and confusing. They were not added by Gilbert Stuart but by someone unknown which is what is meant by "later hand". The names are neither Ricketts nor Breschard. Not even the NGA uses these signatures to indicate who the actual sitter is.

http://www.nga.gov/fcgi-bin/tinfo_f?object=3160
&detail=ins

from the NGA

Inscription

in a later hand, lower left: Portrait of / Mr Rickarts
/ Horse Equestraine [sic] / Friend of the artist /
Gilbert Stuart; in a later hand, lower right: Portrait of
Rickarts / Horse Equestrian / An Intimate Friend of
/ Gilbert Stuarts

These indecipherable inscriptions, added long after the painting was completed by someone other than Gilbert Stuart, are useless in deciding who was the sitter for this portrait.

WEDNESDAY, JANUARY 20, 2010

NON-COMIC STRIPS, ALMOND DIVISION

Many things in life are like lifting a heavy weight. This recipe is one of them. There are two truisms that come to mind whenever I know I'm about to strain every muscle in my body and possibly sustain minor to more than minor injury. Three things actually. One: Avoid injury. Two: lift with your legs. (If you learn anything from all of this, lift with your legs is as good a lesson as any.) But this recipe has nothing to do with these first two thoughts. Mostly. Number three is what concerns us here. Number three, as we all should have learned a long time ago, reads: Before you lift something heavy, know where you're going to put it after you have it in hand. You really don't want to be walking around going, "Where shall I place this awfully heavy object which is causing me such pain as I walk around with it in my hands looking for a place to unload the damn thing other than from where I just picked it up? Ouch."

We are here to avoid that pain. Know what you are going to do with these almondy wonders before you launch into this recipe. Know that you are going to send a dozen to the neighbors. Know that your nieces and nephews will enjoy them without end. Know that your overweight rival in the office will gobble them down and thus be one step closer to taking six months of medical leave due to the triple bypass. Know that the two women sharing the apartment down the hall are going to be just as pleased as punch.

Do not leave these around your own premises. You may keep a half dozen for yourself and a friend. If you do not disperse these immediately you will end up looking like the Pillsbury Doughboy, a sad cross between an adorable adult infant and the guy from the old neighborhood who still lives in his grandparents' basement, is at least 200 pounds overweight and gives off vibes similar to a bad slasher movie.

You have been warned.

½ cup unsalted butter (one stick)

1 3/4 cups all-purpose flour

1 cup sugar

1 egg

2 teaspoons baking powder

½ teaspoon almond extract

a wee bit of milk

½ cup sliced almonds, roughly chopped

Powdered Yet Drippy Sugar Icing

Take the butter and egg out of the refrigerator an hour before you want to make these. You have to get the ingredients in the mood. Warm them up a bit. Ease into it. None of that, "Honey, I'm home, let's do it" shit. Room temperature ingredients. This is the French way.

Preheat oven to 325 degrees.

Beat the crap out of the butter with an electric mixer for about thirty seconds at medium speed. If you don't have an electric mixer, you probably already have massive forearms so I'm not going to help you out.

Toss in 1 cup of flour, all the sugar, your warmed, desirable egg, baking powder, as well as the almond extract. Hit it again with the mixer until completely integrated then toss in the rest of the flour and beat it. Really beat it.

Take this dough and toss it onto a marginally floured cutting board. Chop the dough into four equal parts. Take each one of these and roll it into a twelve inch long roll. You will feel like an idiot but just do it. Take out an ungreased cookie sheet and place the rolls on it about five inches apart. Using the karate chop edge of your hand, flatten the rolls until they're about three inches wide.

Take out your pastry brush (I know, I know), and lightly paint the now flattened rolls with a wee bit of the milky.

Shove that cookie sheet into that 325 oven and let 'er rip for 13 minutes, give or take sixty seconds. When you eyeball these toasted tubes, the edges should be slightly brown, like really over whitened coffee. Take them out of the oven then diagonally slice the suckers into 1 (one) inch(") strips. Cool these babies down on a wire rack (I said, I already know). Drip the disgusting looking icing (recipe follows) all over these puppies. And then get them out of your house.

(Powdered Yet Drippy Sugar Icing - cup powdered sugar, 1/4 teaspoon vanilla, a little milk. Mix sugar, vanilla, and a tablespoon milk together. Add milk a teaspoon at a time until it looks drippingly, disgustingly perfect for slobbering over your almond non-comic strips.)

Then get them out of your house, Doughboy.

MONDAY, JANUARY 18, 2010

BRESCHARD OR RICKETTS?

ONE REASON WHY THIS MATTERS

One of the most important functions of any government is the education of children. A major part of the National Gallery of Art's brief is to aid in the development of America's next generation of citizens. When the government starts disseminating incorrect information to children, and this error is discovered, immediate action should be taken.

Now one might think that Stuart's portrait of a Circus Rider is a small thing. One painting out of hundreds of Stuarts out there. What's the big deal?

follow this link: National Gallery of Art - Gilbert Stuart for Kids

This is the NGA own childrens' guide to Gilbert Stuart. The first painting selected is obvious, The Skater. But the second? Even before the portrait of George Washington! Before the founder of this country! Before Adams, Jefferson, Madison and Monroe! Why it's Breschard, the Circus Rider. Amazing. Before George Washington is Jean Baptiste Breschard, the Circus Rider, Circus Owner, Theatrical Impresario, and a major donor to the first public school in New York City. And, look, there's the story of how Jefferson and Lafayette attended the opening of the Walnut Street Theatre with Breschard. Read it yourself. It's right there in the guide for children.

But wait. That's not the story that's there. And the NGA says that the portrait is of somebody named Ricketts, not Breschard. Instead they tell a story of John Bill Ricketts and George Washington. Probably a true story but it has nothing to do with this painting. It's simply a convenient story which the NGA thinks is as good as any to tell children. The facts of the story may be true, but the reason for it being told isn't factual.

It's not right for the National Gallery of art to spread misinformation to children. Or is it?

SUNDAY, JANUARY 17, 2010

GILBERT STUART'S "JEAN BAPTISTE BRESCHARD, THE CIRCUS RIDER"

In my most recent book, CIRCUS RIDER; a novel history of the first American circus, the identity of the sitter for a Gilbert Stuart portrait is an object of debate. The two contenders for who's who in this piece of early American art history are John Bill Ricketts, an Englishman who brought the first circus to the United States in the 1790s; and Jean Baptiste Breschard, who with his partner, Victor Pépin, captivated the newly liberated colonists with their performances from 1807 until 1815. Traveling a seasonal circuit including New York, Philadelphia, Richmond, Boston and Charleston; Breschard, a Frenchman, and Pépin, a native New Yorker, entertained Americans at their permanent circus theatres with years of sold-out performances including equestrian shows, circus acts, classical drama, melodramas, comic plays, hippodrama and lots, lots, more!

In 1970 the National Gallery of Art renamed this portrait "John Bill Ricketts," disregarding the definitive 1879 identification of the sitter as Jean B. Breschard by George C. Mason (author of The Life and Works of Gilbert Stuart), George Washington Riggs (known as "The President's Banker" and a founder of the Corcoran Museum of Art) and the Museum of Fine Arts, Boston. Mason's book and the Boston Museum's exhibition weren't sufficient evidence for the NGA. Living witnesses to

Breschard's performances weren't enough. Instead they turned to a small note by T. Allston Brown, a gentleman with a reputation for inaccuracy, and changed the name of Stuart's painting from "Breschard, the Circus Rider" to "John Bill Ricketts."

The entire NGA identification rests upon unsupported statements by T. Allston Brown as to who owned the portrait previous to George Washington Riggs. According to Brown the last owner before Mr. Riggs was a certain Peter Grain, a Frenchman and artist. This is the NGA provenance and primary reason for changing the identification. http://www.nga.gov/fcgi-bin/tinfo_f?object=3160 &detail=prov

Oddly enough Peter Grain's son, Peter Grain, Junior, spent most of his professional career working as a scenic director at the Walnut Street Theatre in Philadelphia which was built by Pépin and Breschard. If someone could show that Peter Grain, the elder, was a member of the Circus of Pépin and Breschard, it certainly would go a long way to discrediting the NGA provenance based on the words of T. Allston Brown (This was a man who could publish six factual mistakes within a single paragraph.).

By request of Beth Ahrens-Kley who publishes a Gilbert Stuart blog and is currently researching this particular debate, what follows is fairly definitive proof that Peter Grain was a member of the Circus of Pépin and Breschard. Peter Grain would certainly be capable of identifying his old boss, Jean Baptiste Breschard and passing this information along to George Washington Riggs. This should put an end to any justification for the current NGA stand that the portrait is of Ricketts. Any reasonable institution should once again identify the portrait as Breschard, the Circus Rider.

CIRCUS.

This Evening, Aug. 2, 1809, Messrs. Pepin, & Breshhard, will have the honor to give a brilliant representation of Horsemanship, Vaulting and Dancing.

To which will be added for the first time, the New Pantomine of BILLY, or the Reward of a Good Action, performed with combats, &c. by Mr. P. Grain.——Scene in the adjacent part of a small Village.

Annette, a country girl, Miss Cibert—John Roger, her father, Mr. Simon—Billy, Annette's lover, a simple fellow, Mr. Grain—Francis, do. Mr. Menial—Mourtache, 1st chief of robbers, Mr. Breschard—Rinfort, 2d chief of robbers, Mr. Caytano—Flamant, captain of the military, Mr. Grain—Two Travellers, Messrs. Codet and Allien—An Old Woman, Mr. Fulgence—Soldiers, Robbers, &c.

, Doors to be opened at half past seven o'clock, and the performance to commence precisely at a quarter past eight. Box one dollar—Pit half a dollar—Children half price.　　　　aug. 2

An 1809 advertisement for the Circus of Pépin and Breschard in New York

"This Evening, Aug. 2, 1809, Messrs. Pepin, & Breschard, will have the honor to give a brilliant representation of Horsemanship, Vaulting and Dancing.

To which will be added for the first time the New Pantomime of BILLY, or the Reward of a Good Action, performed with combats, &c. by Mr. P. Grain"

And now from the Walnut Street Theatre: Stuart portrait identified as Breschard! This is only the beginning. It's time to bring back this forgotten piece of history.

CIRCUS RIDER

a novel history of the first American circus

and a great Gilbert Stuart American portrait

SUNDAY, JANUARY 10, 2010

BAD HISTORY

Just for fun I decided to revisit the work of T. Allston Brown, who the National Gallery of Art depends upon greatly for their provenance.

from T. Allston Brown's History of the American Stage, 1870 (nine years after the citation used by the NGA)

Peppin and Burschard. - Peppin and Burschard, with a French Circus, landed in Boston in 1806, from Spain. They performed in conjunction with West, at Philadelphia. Peppin built the Walnut Street Theatre. Peppin had a thorough military education. He was an officer in the cavalry of France. He was born in Albany. His parents were French. They left Albany for Paris when Peppin was two years of age.

http://www.circushistory.org/History/Brown.htm#P

Aside from not knowing how to spell Pépin or Breschard, getting the year they arrived in the USA wrong, 1807 not 1806, Pépin and Breschard together not ever working with West, both Pépin and Breschard building the Walnut Street Theatre in Philadelphia, not Pépin alone, and Mrs. Pépin having never gone to France, I guess the rest of his piece is correct.

For someone who is relied upon as a source for the Smithsonian, getting six facts wrong out of a possible ten is a poor, poor performance.

This is the author the NGA uses to negate Mason, Riggs, and the Museum of Fine Arts, Boston.

breeches, and brass-heeled shoes. Danced for the championship with R. M. Carroll, for $250 a side, at Wallack's Old Theatre, in the presence of a house full, on April 16, 1862, at about 4 P. M. Both men danced well, but the result was a triumph for Peel.

PFEIFFER, OSCAR.—Born in Vienna, Oct. 27, 1830. Made his *debut* in Vienna, in 1844, as a pianist. Made his *debut* in America, in 1850. Revisited America in 1856, and again in 1866.

PEMBERTON, MR.—Born in England. Made his *debut* in 1824, at the Old Chatham Garden, New York, as Bertram.

PENNOYER, AUGUSTUS S.—Born in Monmouth, N. J., June 1, 1829. Commenced his professional career as call boy, at the Old St. Charles Theatre, New Orleans, under the management of Ludlow and Smith. Worked his way up from the ranks, "having filled in his time the positions of property-man, stage carpenter, actor, prompter, stage manager, treasurer, and manager. Joined Peter and Caroline Richings as their agent in the year

profession in New York, at the close of the season of 1867-'68, and has settled down in New York.

PEPITA, SENORITA.—This Spanish *danseuse* made her *debut* in America, April 29, 1863, at the Academy of Music, New York, for the benefit of Mr. Palmo.

PEPPIN AND BURSCHARD.—Peppin and Burschard, with a French Circus, landed in Boston in 1806, from Spain. They performed in conjunction with West, at Philadelphia. Peppin built the Walnut Street Theatre. Peppin had a thorough military education. He was an officer in the cavalry of France. He was born in Albany. His parents were French. They left Albany for Paris when Peppin was two years of age.

PERCY, RITA.—Born in London, Eng., July 15, 1840. At twelve years of age she showed great musical ability, and sang with success at many of the best concerts in the west of England, Ireland and Scotland. After an extensive travelling tour as a vocalist, she appeared on the stage in London as a bur-

SATURDAY, JANUARY 9, 2010

MORE GOVERNMENTAL ERRORS

(In reply to an inquiry.)

As has been mentioned, Peter Grain worked in the Circus of Pépin and Breschard. At the moment I'm looking at an image of an 1809 newspaper notice. P. Grain's drama "Billy" is advertised by Pépin and Breschard and Grain has the leading role. Grain was a member of the company for at least a year. Having worked with Jean Breschard, I feel comfortable in assuming Grain would be capable of recognizing a portrait of his former boss.

You should look into exactly who George Washing Riggs was. Among other things he was probably the richest man in the United States during his time, an advisor to Presidents, and one of the founders of the most prestigious Corcoran Gallery of Art in Washington, D.C. It was he who identified the sitter to Mason. In my files is a copy of a handwritten note from Riggs to Mason identifying the portrait as being that of Breschard.

Pépin and Breschard were the premiere performers in the U.S. from 1808 until 1815. (Very few people in this country can name the most popular performers of any decade during the 19th century.) Calling either of them a minor circus equestrian shows poor scholarship on someone's part. Some research into historical newspapers will prove an education on this point. The NGA has been professionally negligent about this.

Ricketts's brother being the first owner of this particular painting is a misreading of an extremely dubious source. This attribution is at best a rumor and at worst, well, never mind. This is by far the weakest part of the NGA provenance and does not rise to meet any academic standard.

When someone is in the entertainment business, there are numerous reasons why one would wish their portrait painted.

M indicates that Ricketts left for the West Indies before the painting was finished. This is without any factual basis. A Mr. C at the NGA had serious doubts about the Ricketts ID in the late 60s (I'd have to look at my notes for a more precise date), his research into the identification was a bit shallow since, I believe, the NGA is basically more interested in the portrait being by Stuart than in exactly who the sitter is.

FRIDAY, JANUARY 8, 2010

BRESCHARD, THE CIRCUS RIDER

BY GILBERT STUART

In 2004, thanks to the wonders of Google, a portrait of Jean Baptiste Breschard by Gilbert Stuart became known to me. Having only discovered the existence of this historical Breschard a few years previous, I was intrigued. Unfortunately, the name of this particular painting was no longer "Breschard, the Circus Rider," the sitter was now designated as "John Bill Ricketts," the portrait's identification being changed by the National Gallery of Art sometime in the 1970s.

After having completed a great deal of research and having read pertinent parts of the NGA archive, I became convinced by the existing evidence that in all probability the portrait by Gilbert Stuart was indeed that of Jean Baptiste Casmiere Breschard.

So I wrote a book about the man, the circus, the artist, the painting, the NGA, etc.. I'm presently in the process of having it published.

The main reason I'm writing this is due to the fact that another student of Stuart has come across the controversy and is using some of the entries I've helped edit in Wikipedia as sources for posts to her blog. All I can say is that like all encyclopedias, Wikipedia doesn't contain all the facts, and if I can be of any help, let me know.

WEDNESDAY, JANUARY 6, 2010

PARTIAL LIST OF DEMOCRATIC PARTY FAILURES IN PAST YEAR

-Failure to prosecute those United States officials who authorized the torture of prisoners and those US agents and mercenaries who actually performed those criminal acts. This failure to prosecute may itself be a criminal act.

-More than doubling the amount of troops and mercenaries in Afghanistan.

-To this day, a failure to reduce the number of troops in Iraq.

-Failure to close Guantanamo.

-Failure to bring single payer healthcare up for debate in Congress and Obama's failure to campaign for a public option or similar method of health care insurance.

-Endorsing a mandatory purchase of private insurance by US citizens. This is probably unconstitutional.

-Continuation of a "never ending" war policy.

For myself, the Green Party has now become the only organized political party worth backing.

MONDAY, JANUARY 4, 2010

VOTED MOST POPULAR

Now that Obama's poll numbers are in the pits, how long will it be before some new major military action suddenly pops up? Will it simply be a variation on the ongoing misadventure in Afghanistan or will the head of the Democratic Party want a war all his own? I sincerely hope I'm wrong on this one. Wouldn't it be nice if the "Larynx from the Loop" didn't disappoint for a change. His list of failures is getting to be a bit too long. Let's all hope

more people aren't killed for the political expediency of another party.

SATURDAY, JANUARY 2, 2010

AMATEURS

Over the past few months I've had the occasion to witness more than two local area amateur art presentations. At times I have been amused, awed, confused, disappointed, annoyed, and many of the other states in which one finds oneself when presented with performances not advertised as being anyway professional.

Overall they were certainly worth every penny I paid and for the most part were an enjoyable way to spend an evening, sometimes needing to leave the performance itself aside, and concentrate on the social aspects which accompany these mostly under rehearsed presentations.

Which leads to the subjects of criticism, satire, racism, elitism, and free-fire zones.

Let's start with the definition of a free-fire zone since it is the simplest to explain and where the greatest consensus should be discovered. My standard for a FFZ is simple and elegant. If a performer takes cash money from the public, they may be fired upon at will. As with most things, exceptions abound. Nominal sums collected for charities of one type or another, along with obviously non-professional performers are given a pass. But even if the toll at the door is minimal, if the company makes any claims to being professionals, they may be shot on sight if the infraction demands such punishment.

In short, take my money, expect my wrath if you step onto the stage under prepared.

But we are discussing amateurs. Lovers of the arts. Is it elitism not to criticize their performances? Not at all. If fact it is a far, far better thing to ignore an amateur performance than to employ either a condescending or uncritical eye to such shows.

Racism. Not exactly but try this for a moment. How should sportswriters sum up the Special Olympics? Should they compare the competitors to actual Olympians? Of course not. Should they ink yard by yard coverage of each thrilling race? Maybe if there is a thrill here or there but that's probably not the best way to go. Or should they simply gloss over the whole event and eventually proclaim that a good time was had by all and everyone enjoyed a day out in the sunshine and fresh air. You can probably guess where I side on this one.

Which leads to another annoyance. There has been a trend of late by professional entertainers to satirize amateur performers and under talented professionals. This is the equivalent of grammar school punks mocking a schoolmate's lisp. It's right up there with Special Olympic's jokes. Where is the art in creating mediocre art in order to mock untalented performers? What pride can be taken in attempting to capture the essence of a failed performance? It's a race to the bottom.

What these professional entertainers are achieving is the distancing of their audience from the object of their ridicule. In order to be entertained by such rubbish, you have to view these objects as not being like yourself. As being the other. As in "even though I'm a thirteen year-old idiot, at least I'm better than anyone who lisps." It's dehumanizing another human being. It's the old minstrel show. It's the same technique as racism.

Satire should only be used on objects in need of attack. If you think your amateur theatrical group is in need of attack, you need serious help.

Public criticism should be reserved for those who seek assessment on a professional level. Amateurs perform for the love of the work. Those who mock amateurs are in it, at best, only for the money.

SUNDAY, DECEMBER 27, 2009

PEANUT BUTTER MOOSEY COOKIES

1 cup peanut butter

1 cup butter, at room temperature

2 cups packed brown sugar

2 eggs

2 teaspoons pure vanilla extract

½ teaspoon salt

1 teaspoon baking soda

1 teaspoon baking powder

preheat oven to 350 degrees

Cream the peanut butter, butter, and brown sugar until light and well blended. Beat in the eggs one at a time. Stir in the vanilla. Sift together the flour, salt, baking soda, and baking powder. Gently fold the dry ingredients into the wet ingredients. Roll ½ tablespoons full of dough between your palms to form 1-inch balls and place them 2 inches apart on the baking sheets. Bake for 10 minutes. Transfer the cookies to a rack to cool.

WEDNESDAY, DECEMBER 23, 2009

BREAKFAST SERVICES AT BARB'S DINER

"Hey, these numbers can't be right." Phil steps up to the counter as he inspects the stats one more time. "No way, not for a kid his age."

"Some kids got it. Some don't. He's got it. He's got a lot of it." George rearranges scrambled eggs on his plate. "They'll gobble him up in no time flat. Probably be playing the Bigs before he's eighteen."

Phil waves down the woman working behind the counter then parks his butt on a stool next to his partner. She moves into position, and braces both men. "Barb, hey, how's 'bout some of your excellent waffles this fine morning?" Nodding, she scribbles notes in her pad. "Coffee, one of these bad boys," he points out a particular cruller beneath a plastic dome perched on the Formica counter, "and let's have some cranberry juice this morning. Hey, just for the hell of it. I'm feeling 'venturous today."

"Sure, hon." Barb rips a sheet from her pad and then impales it on the kitchen/counter passthrough spike. She slaps the bell, awakening Bernie, "The Chef". She pours Phil his java then shouts over her shoulder to the kitchen "Rise and shine, sweety pie, you can sleep when you're dead."

Bernie is moving and cooking before he's aware he's awake. He always answers the call. He tosses frozen waffles into the toaster, then sits himself down for another catnap. Dreams of southern climes and playing ball with his buddies flood Bernie's mind. He needs the rest. This isn't his only job.

"Take a kid like this guy we're talking about," George borrows Phil's newspaper. As he sips his brew, George marks notes around the article, "twenty years ago, he would've been doing what? Running cross-country?"

"Yeah, maybe baseball." Phil's half-eaten cruller rests in one hand while he brushes crumbs from the front of his zip-up jacket with the other. "Forget football, not enough meat on his bones. Forget basketball, too short. Hockey? Hey, get real. That leaves track and baseball. Yeah, cross-country or shortstop. Looks the type to me."

"And they play the damn game just about all year round. Who would have thought?"

"Here you go, hon." Barb parks a waffled filled plate and set-ups on Phil's place mat, "Anything else?"

"Hey, did I already drink my cranberry juice?"

"Sorry, Phil. You know how I get." Turning her back to the partners, Barb pours cranberry juice as she takes an order over her shoulder from a customer who's just come in and taken a seat.

"How ya doin' this mornin', hon?"

Barb delivers the order. "Happy now, Phil?"

"Couldn't be more delighted." He sips his juice. "Hey, how's your boy these days? Staying out of trouble?"

Barb's tired face lightens a bit. "Thanks for askin', hon. Who knows with kids his age? I haven't caught him at it again and the cops haven't either. So knock wood."

George motions for more coffee. "He should play sports. Keep him away from bad elements." Both George and Phil laugh. "Seriously, what's he now, thirteen, fourteen?"

"Thirteen."

"That's plenty young. Get him out of the apartment. Away from those damn computer games. Or worse. Get him out running around playing in fresh air. Supervised." George polishes off his eggs. "He like any particular sport?"

"Nothing I know anything about."

"What you mean, Barb?" Now it's Phil's turn for more coffee. "It's Spring. I know a couple of teams he might be able to play on. Hey, didn't he play Little League a couple of seasons?"

Barb rests her elbows on the counter and her head in her hands. "Forget it. He never liked baseball. The way he played, I can't blame him. He kills time watching soccer now and then. That's about as active as he gets."

Both Phil and George groan at the mention of soccer.

"Hey, Georgie, got somethin' for me?" Walking into Barb's small diner, Charlie C is all smiles.

George matches him, grin for grin. "Of course, Charlie, had yourself a good night last night. Didn't you." George looks to Phil who slides an envelope to his partner. "Who you like today?"

"Not today, Georgie. Sorry. Today I've got to cash out and run. Kids I coach need some new uniforms."

The light bulb inside the lamp Phil maintains in the recesses of his mind for illuminating brilliant ideas switches on. "Hey, still coachin' middle school, Charlie boy?"

"Yeah, Phil, ten to fourteen. I actually do some real good work with kids that age. Any older and their life's already pretty much set in stone." George hands Charlie C bills from the envelope. "Thanks, Georgie. I like workin' with kids. Keeps them from sitting in front of stupid electronic screens all day, playing video games instead of actually living."

"Not soccer is it?" Phil hopes against hope.

Charlie C cracks another grin. "Sure is, Phil, soccer. Soccer, football, whatever you want to call it." Charlie C calls out to the cook in the back. "Right, Bernardo? Football, Bernie, football. Gooooooooooal!"

From his station behind the diner's wall Bernardo chimes the call bell three times and shouts out enthusiastically, "Football!"

"Football, soccer, I don't care." Phil signals Barb, who by now has drifted off to tend other customers, to come back. "Hey, Charlie, you know Barb's kid, right?"

"Can't say I've seen him in a couple of years."

Barb joins the conversation. "Mornin', Charlie C, get ya somethin'?"

"No thanks, hon. I've got to get my rear in gear. Just now Phil mentioned your boy. Haven't seen him for a while. How's he been doin'?"

"Thanks for askin', hon. He's doin' O.K., I guess. Usual kids' stuff."

Phil catches Charlie C's eye, urging him on.

"Listen, Barb, I'm coachin' a soccer team for the parish and I need some more players. How old's the boy?"

"Thirteen."

"Perfect. How's about I give him a call later tonight and see if he wants to play on my team?"

For the first time all morning, someone smiles a smile of actual joy. "Charlie, that would be great. Let me write down the number for ya." Taking the pencil from behind her ear, Barb again scribbles in her pad. Handing the note to Charlie C, for a moment, a simple moment, their eyes meet.

Neither George nor Phil miss seeing that.

"Good man, Charlie C." George toasts him with his coffee cup. "We'll be seeing you later in the week then?"

"Sure." As Charlie C starts to leave, he looks toward Barb again and stops. "What the hell, Georgie, I'm feeling lucky this morning. Put me down for half a hundred on the Tigers."

George nods, Phil gives a quick wave, Barb's smile gets even wider, and Charlie C hits the street.

"Refills, boys? On the house." George and Phil both tap their coffee cups for more. Barb tops them off and moves on to other customers.

"Soccer. I'll never get it." George bemoans the changing times.

"So it's not our sport, George, no big deal. Adapt and move on. Hey, that's what I always say. That's my motto."

"Yeah, I guess you're right. I'll tell you one thing and it ain't two, Phil."

"What's that, George?"

"The public is never going to get the kind of service we deliver from those damn internet bookmakers. No way, no how. I'll tell you that. They can't deliver our kind of service."

"You're damn straight, George. Hey, they can't beat the personal touch."

With that, the two bookies finish their coffees. They've more work to do and other stops to make.

As the partners leave the diner, Bernie the cook awakens from another catnap dream of green fields and soccer balls. "Goooooooooooal!!!!!"

END

from IN THE WIND by Peter Breschard

A FINE BELGIAN ALE RECIPE

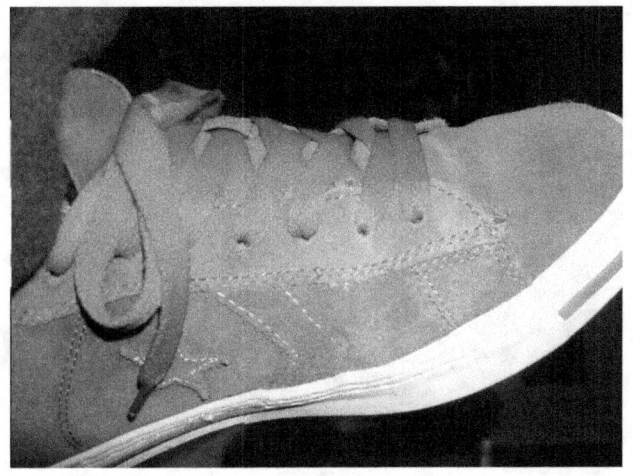

1 pound 40 Lovibond caramel malt

8.25 pounds pale liquid malt extract

2 ounces Cascade hop pellets, boil 1 hour

2 ounces Cascade hop pellets

4.2 ounces orange peel

3 chamomile teabags

Wyeast 1214 Belgian Ale or White Labs WLP530
Abbey Ale

If you don't know what to do with these, let me
know.

MONDAY, DECEMBER 21, 2009

A LETTER TO THE EDITOR

Dear Editor,

I find it deeply offensive that Creationism is not being taught in our schools. Of course the Creationism of which I speak is not the Christian Creationism, it is the Zachooly Creationism passed down to all Zachoolyists in the sacred scrolls of our religion. As is taught in our most enlightened faith, the earth was created by the wise Mistress Zachooly on the third evening of the second day of her journey through the magic forest of Zaab. All of this is well documented in the holy writings. Christian Creationism and the Creationist truths of all religions should be offered in our public schools, along with the true Creation teachings of the Mistress God Zachooly and her group of elfin warriors. Science, on the other hand, may well be an entirely different kettle of fish. Enjoy the upcoming lengthening of the day.

Peter Breschard

Okemos, MI

SUNDAY, DECEMBER 20, 2009